This I Believe:

THE LIVING PHILOSOPHIES
OF ONE HUNDRED THOUGHTFUL
MEN AND WOMEN IN ALL WALKS
OF LIFE —— AS WRITTEN FOR
AND WITH A FOREWORD BY

EDWARD R. MURROW

Edited by EDWARD P. MORGAN

SIMON AND SCHUSTER

NEW YORK · 1952

PRINTED IN THE UNITED STATES OF AMERICA
BY AMERICAN BOOK—STRATFORD PRESS, INC., NEW YORK

To
MARGOT TREVOR WHEELOCK
who was responsible for *This I Believe*.
She chose Joseph Fort Newton's creed as hers,
and lived it.

❧§❧

"We must take time, take pains, have a plan, form spiritual habits, if we are to keep our souls alive; and now is the time to begin. A man to whom religion is a reality, and who knows what is meant by 'the practice of salvation,' keeps his balance, because the living center of his life is spiritual. He cannot be upset, nor shaken. The same hard knocks come to him as to others, but he reacts to them by the central law of his life. He suffers deeply, but he does not sour. He knows frustration, but he goes right on in his kindness and faith. He sees his own shortcomings but he does not give up, because a power rises up from his spiritual center and urges him to the best."

Joseph Fort Newton

EASTER 1949

Foreword

IN THE AUTUMN of 1940, when Britain stood alone, when the bombers came at dusk each evening and went away at dawn, I observed a sign on a church just off the East India Dock Road; it was crudely lettered and it read. "If your knees knock, kneel on them." I quoted that sign in a broadcast to America that night, but did not fully understand it. For even in those dark days I could observe no more kneeling or knocking knees than at the time of the Anschluss or Munich. The imminence of disaster brought no spiritual revival. And yet, at a time when most men save Englishmen despaired of England's life, there was a steadiness, a confidence and determination that must have been based on something other than a lack of imagination.

As the months wore on, and the nights lengthened, and the casualty lists mounted, I became more concerned to try to understand what sustained this island people· what belief or what mythology caused them to stand so steady in their shoes. In part, it was ignorance of their own weakness; in part, it was a reluctance to appear obvious by expressing doubt as to the ultimate outcome. But at bottom this calm confidence stemmed from a belief that what they were defending was good; that Englishmen had devised a system of regulating the relationship between the individual and the state which was superior to all others, and which would survive even though cold military calculations concluded that the state was doomed.

There was little logic in this British belief. Unconsciously, they dug deep into their history and felt that Drake, Raleigh, Frobisher, Hawkins, Cromwell and all the rest were looking down at them, and they were obliged to appear worthy in the eyes of their ancestors. But above everything else, they believed. They believed not only in themselves but that they were fighting against evil things and the fight was worth while.

No democracy has been nearer the fire and survived than was Britain in that long winter. And one reason for survival was that the nation did not betray the things in which it believed. After Italy entered the war, one of the few murder cases to reach the Law Lords on appeal was decided An Italian citizen, long resident in Britain, had been convicted by the lower courts of killing a British seaman in Soho. The high court reversed the verdict, set the Italian free, and in the pubs, and in Parliament, on the buses, and in newspaper offices this was regarded as the normal functioning of British justice.

At a time when German bombers were coming through in the daylight over London, when the Germans were expected on the beaches the first foggy morning, the House of Commons, which might have been destroyed with all its members by one well-placed enemy bomb, devoted two days to discussing the conditions under which enemy aliens were being held on the Isle of Man. For the House of Commons was determined that, though the Island fell, there would be nothing resembling concentration camps in Britain, and the rights under law of enemy aliens would not be abused. That is what the British collectively believed.

No man can measure or transmit the degree or detail of another man's belief. But it is possible on occasion to report it. The night after the Munich agreement was signed, I sat with Jan Masaryk, the Czechoslovak Ambassador, in his London embassy. It was the anniversary of his father's death. We had finished a broadcast to America at four in the morning; we both felt that the Munich agreement meant that war was inevitable. But Jan believed that somehow, some way, the forces of evil would be defeated. Speaking of Hitler and Mussolini, he said· "I assure you, God will not let two such heathens control Europe" His belief, at that time, was greater than my own.

Nearly six years later, when we entered that foul concentration camp of Buchenwald with bodies still stacked in the courtyard, I discovered that the hatred of Czech for Czech, Pole for Pole, was much greater than their hatred for their German captors and butchers. For they believed, these miserable, emaciated Czechs and Poles, in different things; their faith in the future of their country walked down different roads. It was the hatred of Communist for non-Communist, and there was no room for compromise. They believed in different things, and even the imminence of death and the ties of common citizenship could not break that difference in belief. I saw that same thing later in the first summer of the war in Korea when South Korean troops refused to obey the orders of American commanders to withdraw, although both their flanks were exposed. They believed in the cause for which they were fighting; and they fought and believed until they were overrun and killed. It was a difference in belief in the things regarded as worth being killed for that divided the Czechs and Poles in the concentration camps, that divided the North and South Koreans.

I would suppose that men believe what they believe as a result of inheritance, indoctrination, the number of calories they are able to consume, the climate in which they live, the ideas they acquire from others. No route map can be drawn showing how an individual has reached the beliefs he now holds. No man can draw a chart for another which will lead that other to tranquil and tenable beliefs. Conversely, there is no road block that cannot be surmounted or by-passed by the active mind determined to follow the truth wherever it may lead him. And there is as yet no law preventing a man from defending what he believes, although civilized social intercourse requires that he respect the beliefs of those who disagree with him.

I have been a reporter for much of my adult life, using the instruments of radio and television. But these are mass media where the speaker is remote from his audience. It is rather like putting letters in a rusty mail box and never being sure that anyone comes to collect them. The job of a reporter who can never see the eyes of his listeners is to provide information upon which opinion and belief can be based. The only way of discovering what people believe is to ask them. We have discovered in preparing this series of statements that most people have never attempted to reduce to writing what they believe and why. Almost without exception they have told us that this is the most difficult piece of composition they have undertaken—to say, in a few hundred words, what they believe to be the important and permanent landmarks they have found in their journey so far upon this minor planet.

There was a time in this and other countries when sermons by great preachers and editorials by distinguished editors were the subject of prolonged and considered discussion in social gatherings. There was also a time when the writing of letters was an art so well developed that some of the letters were worth keeping and later being published between covers. But the speed of modern communication has largely turned conversation into assertion, and letter-writing into telegrams. The reporter and the listener, or the reader, are overrun and smothered, trampled down by the newest event before they can gain perspective on the one that just passed by. It has become a cliché to say that modern man has been debased and materialized by the circumstances of his daily life.

We do, it is true, live in a society that is materialistic and mechanistic, where most of the goods we use are mass produced. We employ the same phrases, buy nationally advertised products, wear nationally branded hats and suits; the majority of newspaper editors have abdicated to the syndicated columns. The voice of one broadcaster is heard from one end of the country to the other. There exists a real danger that the right of dissent, the right to be wrong, may be swamped because the instruments of communication are too closely held. We face the risk of forgetting that today's minority may become tomorrow's majority, and that every majority in a free society today was not so long ago a minority.

The matter of what men believe became of great importance to me when I first discovered that a friend of mine had been killed, not because of what he had done, but because he insisted upon retaining and agitating for his beliefs. I have known many men who have traveled many roads that brought them to beliefs ranging from Catholicism to Communism. I have never yet heard a man express what he believed in a fashion that failed to interest me. Most of the contributions in this book reflect an abiding belief in the importance and the inviolability of the individual spirit; they reflect a belief in the dignity of the individual and the conviction that any belief worthy of an individual must be hammered out by that individual on the anvil of experience and cannot be packaged and delivered by print, radio, or television.

Occasionally in recent times there has occurred something which has underlined and re-emphasized the independence of the individual and the mystery of what he believes and how he reaches that belief. It happened in England in the late war; it happened with many people with faith enough to regard their beliefs as more important than their lives.

This volume is no publishers' effort to tell you what you should believe. It is rather a compilation of experience and incident which may help you to recognize some of the signposts that have been meaningful to others.

For my own part, I remain fascinated by the manner and method by which people reach their beliefs and, at the same time, gratified by the demonstrable fact that their beliefs are not predictable. Four years ago, in the 1948 Presidential campaign, many of us, reporters, readers and listeners alike, were enthralled by something that wasn't true. The pollsters told us what we would do. We almost came to believe that the hopes, the fears, the prejudices, the aspirations of the people who live on this great continent could be neatly measured and pigeonholed, figured out with a slide rule. As individuals we didn't count; we were just little dots on a graph. The pollsters turned out to be wrong, we were not predictable, and regardless of the political consequences, their error restored to each of us a little dignity and some mystery as to why we believe what we do. This experience re-emphasized the importance and the inscrutability of the individual. We are not predictable, we are not robots. The individual is unpredictable, and in the area of what he believes, he is still sovereign.

At a time when the tide runs toward a shore of conformity, when dissent is often confused with subversion, when a man's belief may be subject to investigation as well as his action, we have thought it useful to present these brief statements by people who have attempted to define what it is that they believe.

EDWARD R. MURROW

Contents

EDWARD R. MURROW: FOREWORD   vii

WARD WHEELOCK: *The Power of an Idea*   xvii

ह‍ॐ

ROBERT G. ALLMAN· *A Ball to Roll Around*   1

LIONEL BARRYMORE. *Does Anybody Believe an Actor?*   3

DR. SAMUEL M. BEST: *How to Give Your Money Away*   5

CARROLL BINDER: *About Secrets and Falling Tiles*   7

ALEXANDER BLOCH: *Life in a Violin Case*   9

ELMER H BOBST: *Man Is Like a Fruit Tree*   11

DR. EDMUND A. BRASSET: *The Invisible Medicine of Humanity*   13

LEE HASTINGS BRISTOL· *Paying the Rent of Service*   15

INA CORINNE BROWN: *What Are People Good For?*   17

JULIEN BRYAN: *Friendship Is a Passport*   19

PEARL BUCK: *Roll Away the Stone*   21

JAMES B. CAREY: *Flotsam, Jetsam and Liberty*   23

CARROLL CARROLL: *Dreams Are the Stuff Life Is Made Of*   25

SIR HUGH CASSON: *Keep the Innocent Eye*   27

GENERAL LUCIUS D. CLAY: *The Creed of a Soldier*   29

SUSAN COBBS· *Causes Are People*   31

NORMAN COUSINS: *A Game of Cards*   33

LOU R. CRANDALL: *A Straight Wall Is Hard to Build*   35

ELMER DAVIS: *Freedom Is Worth the Risk*   37

J FRANK DOBIE: *What Makes Me Feel Big*   39

BOBBY DOERR. *I Don't Play to the Grandstand*   41

WILLIAM O. DOUGLAS: *My Father's Evening Star*   43

CAROLINE DUER: *White Is Made of Many Colors*   45

JAMES Q. DU PONT: *A Lesson Learned at Midnight*   47

CONTENTS

DAME EDITH EVANS: *What Does God Say to Me?* 49

DR. FRED DOW FAGG, JR.: *Spiritual Handholds on Life* 51

PAT FRANK *I Am Happy with My Time* 53

J. GEORGE FREDERICK: *The Law of the Heart* 55

LUCY FREEMAN: *A Mask Was Stifling Me* 57

DR NELSON GLUECK: *Discovery in a Thunderstorm* 59

WARD GREENE: *A Sort of Unselfish Selfishness* 61

JOYCE GRENFELL: *The Art of Bouncing Back* 63

HELEN HAYES. *A Morning Prayer in a Little Church* 65

GENERAL LEWIS B. HERSHEY: *We Can't Just Play with Spools* 67

ANNE HEYWOOD. *Do You Know Your Special Talent?* 69

ROBERT HILLYER: *Escape the Dark Destructive Force* 71

NAT HOLMAN: *You Cannot "Fix" a Real Faith* 73

HERBERT HOOVER· *I See No Doom Down an Alley* 75

LEWIS M. HOSKINS *The Hole in the Enemy's Armor* 77

JOHN HUGHES: *Taxi Drivers Are People Too* 79

ALDOUS HUXLEY: *Learning to Get Out of the Way* 81

C. JARED INGERSOLL: *The Soundest Investment of All* 83

DR DAVID DALLAS JONES· *Fixing Up the Run-Down Places* 85

CAPTAIN LLOYD JORDAN *Revelations on a Bomb Run* 87

HELEN KELLER: *The Light of a Brighter Day* 89

ANDRE KOSTELANETZ. *Matisse and the Music of Discontent* 91

OLGA KOUSSEVITZKY: *I Beseech You to Look* 93

DR MAX T. KRONE: *John Donne Was Right* 95

MRS. JOHN G LEE: *Inspiration from a Drainpipe* 97

HERBERT H. LEHMAN. *The Only Way to Make a Friend* 99

C. DAY LEWIS. *I Wish I Could Believe* 101

DAVID LOTH· *Diogenes Didn't Need a Lamp* 103

LILLIAN BUENO McCUE: *Three O'Cat Is Still Game* 105

RICHARD H. McFEELY: *The Vital Human Difference* 107

DR. ROBERT M. MacIVER. *The Strange and Wonderful Thing* 109

MRS. MARTY MANN: *Twice I Sought Death* 111

xiv

THOMAS MANN: *Life Grows in the Soil of Time*   113

MARGARET MEAD: *A New Control of Destiny*   115

LAURITZ MELCHIOR: *A Touch of God's Finger*   117

JOE J. MICKLE: *An Optimist Pleads Guilty*   119

DIMITRI MITROPOULOS: *The Debt of the Artist*   121

NEWBOLD MORRIS: *The Hidden Vitality of Human Beings*   123

PROF. GILBERT MURRAY: *The Greeks Had an Answer*   125

ALBERT J. NESBITT: *How to Refill an Empty Life*   127

BONARO W. OVERSTREET: *The Law of Shared Investment*   129

PROF. HARRY A OVERSTREET. *The Hidden World Around Us*   131

SAUL K. PADOVER: *A Shining Day Will Come*   133

ANNE PHIPPS *Growing in the Middle Ground*   135

RALPH PINELLI: *I Call Things As I See Them*   137

BENTZ PLAGEMANN *Destination Through Darkness*   139

DICK POWELL: *A Man's Will to His Son*   141

J. ARTHUR RANK: *The Wisdom of a King*   143

ROSE RESNICK: *One Girl Changed My Life*   145

QUENTIN REYNOLDS: *If I Were a Dictator*   147

RALPH RICHMOND: *A New Look from Borrowed Time*   149

JACKIE ROBINSON: *Free Minds and Hearts at Work*   151

ANNE M. ROMBEAU: *My Faith Is Like a Circle*   153

MRS. ELEANOR ROOSEVELT. *Growth That Starts from Thinking*   155

VIRGINIA SALE: *Don't Step Out of Character*   157

RICHARD SALMON: *I Do a Lot of Office Fishing*   159

DR. LEON J. SAUL· *Suffering Is Self-Manufactured*   161

EVA R. SAXL: *I Never Stopped Believing*   163

DORE SCHARY: *The World's Greatest Force*   165

WILLIAM B. SEARS: *Closer Than My Own Back Yard*   167

LOUIS B. SELTZER· *Personal Inventory by Appointment*   169

WILLIAM L. SHIRER. *A Reporter Quotes His Sources*   171

WALLACE STEGNER: *Everything Potent Is Dangerous*   173

CONTENTS

LELAND STOWE: *You Have to Water the Plant*   175
CHARLES P. TAFT: *Attuning the Listening Ear*   177
DR. HAROLD TAYLOR *Give Part of Yourself Away*   179
ALICE THOMPSON: *I Live Four Lives at a Time*   181
ELIZABETH GRAY VINING. *My World Was Wrecked Once*   183
CONSTANCE WARREN: *What Would Christ Have Done?*   185
REBECCA WEST: *Goodness Doesn't Just Happen*   187
JOE WILLIAMS: *Baseball Has a Religion Too*   189
MEREDITH WILLSON: *Maxie's Recipe for Happiness*   191
PEGGY WOOD: *Two Commandments Are Enough*   193
GEORGE YOUNG: *Philosophy from a Tugboat*   195
DARRYL F. ZANUCK: *Walk Clean around the Hill*   197
WILLIAM ZORACH: *The Thread of Permanence*   199

The Power of an Idea

SUPPOSE YOU could sit down every day for 100 days with some deeply thoughtful man or woman, a different one each day, while he opened his heart and mind to you. As he talked, you'd learn what were his inmost beliefs, how he arrived at them, and how they have influenced his life.

You would consider that an exciting experience, would you not, a rare privilege? Beyond that, you would find it helpful in formulating your own personal beliefs, in arriving at your own sense of values —to the enrichment of your own life. Well, here you have that opportunity.

For this book is the summation of an idea at once so simple, so basic, and apparently desired by so many people that it has exploded wherever anyone has taken the time to listen, to read and think. If ever a book were published by popular demand, this is it. Thousands of people, including hundreds of educators and no fewer than sixteen publishers, after hearing "This I Believe" on the air or reading it in the newspapers, wrote in to urge its appearance between covers.

"This I Believe" began—and continues—as a radio program. It is broadcast in the United States 2200 separate times each week from 196 of the most powerful radio stations. It reaches 39,000,000 people in this country alone—on an average of twice a week. This makes it the most listened-to radio program in the world. It is broadcast 900 times a week on 150 stations abroad, and over the "Voice of America" weekly in six languages. It reaches our men and women of the armed forces in Korea, in Germany, and around the world daily. In addition, newspapers in this country carry "This I Believe" some 8,500,-000 times weekly—it appears once a week in 85 leading dailies. The State Department is currently offering it abroad to the most important papers in every country with which diplomatic relations are maintained—some 97 countries. It is being used regularly in hundreds of schools and classrooms. And yet—to paraphrase a once-famous radio line—this is only the beginning.

Let me tell you how it started.

"This I Believe" was launched in 1949 at a business luncheon of four men. The conversation began with the truism that among people generally material values were gaining and spiritual values declining. The reasons were obvious: the uncertainty of the economic future, the shadow of war, the atom bomb, army service for one's self or loved ones, the frustration of young people facing the future. Seldom has there been a time when an inventory of one's personal beliefs and sense of values seemed to be more needed. For the individual's credo contains the seeds of the strength and happiness of the family, the community and the nation.

What could be done? The group of four decided to start "This I Believe." It was planned to have a chosen number of men and women unfold their personal philosophy, tell what they deem important in life, and give the personal rules by which they run their own lives—in a 5-minute radio program daily, and a 600-word newspaper article weekly. Edward R. Murrow, one of the men at the luncheon, agreed to introduce the guests—business men, lawyers, physicians, writers, educators, baseball players, actors—men and women of many races, colors and faiths, people known and unknown, people in all walks of life, but all successful in their chosen profession and in their adjustment to life and living.

"This I Believe" has no connection with any church—it is run by laymen. Each personal philosophy is of spiritual significance—it touches directly or indirectly upon the basic principles taught by every church. Yet there are 75,000,000 people in the United States not associated with any church and this book is for them too.

What is the purpose of the book? Of what practical value is it? How can it serve you? It is obvious that the most important job any person has to do is to run his own life. Everyone has the responsibility of developing his talents, his knowledge, his understanding in order to contribute to the work of the world in some way. But beyond this, his whole life, that which constitutes him, is based on his beliefs. These need not be religious only, or even majorly, though faith in a Supreme Being usually forms a part of the creed of most thinking people. But they are the cornerstone of daily living—the answer to the question, "How can I help myself to a fuller, happier and more contented life?" Too many people never do find the answer to this question.

I believe this has been the hardest to write of any book I know. A hundred people of character have searched within themselves and tried to tell you honestly what they found. This is hard to do, and many of the writers are themselves dissatisfied with their telling. So to you, the reader, I say: Try always to see not just the words, but to see through them—to the meaning beyond

The beliefs of the men and women in this book—of anyone—will change importantly over the years Very positive beliefs of young people change through experience, so that in later years they look back and say, "How could I have thought that so important?" But this is natural and good. The only wrong is in not letting your beliefs grow as you grow. For example, the beliefs presented here range in point of age from those of a twenty-year-old girl student looking forward to life—a promising one—to those of a former President of the United States, who at 78 looks back on life—a full one.

Thousands of books have been written on the subject of "What is my place in the world?"—"What are my obligations?"—"Why should I live and how?" Most of these have been exhortations or preachments or special pleadings, ending in "You must do this or else!" "This I Believe" sells nothing. It asks nothing. It seeks only to stimulate—and to help.

This is a book for the home bedside and for the soldier's knapsack, for reading and for pondering. It will fail of its purpose if it does not open your mind and suggest that you try charting your own belief. It will succeed if it does. Thousands have dug deep and found gold. May you do likewise!

WARD WHEELOCK

This I Believe

A Ball to Roll Around

BY ROBERT G. ALLMAN

I LOST my sight when I was four years old by falling off a box car in
a freight yard in Atlantic City and landing on my head. Now I am
thirty-two. I can vaguely remember the brightness of sunshine and
what color red is. It would be wonderful to see again, but a calamity
can do strange things to people. It occurred to me the other day that
I might not have come to love life as I do if I hadn't been blind. I
believe in life now. I am not so sure that I would have believed in it
so deeply, otherwise. I don't mean that I would prefer to go without
my eyes. I simply mean that the loss of them made me appreciate
the more what I had left.

Life, I believe, asks a continuous series of adjustments to reality.
The more readily a person is able to make these adjustments, the
more meaningful his own private world becomes. The adjustment
is never easy I was bewildered and afraid. But I was lucky. My parents and my teachers saw something in me—a potential to live, you
might call it—which I didn't see, and they made me want to fight it
out with blindness.

The hardest lesson I had to learn was to believe in myself. That
was basic. If I hadn't been able to do that, I would have collapsed
and become a chair rocker on the front porch for the rest of my life.
When I say belief in myself I am not talking about simply the kind
of self-confidence that helps me down an unfamiliar staircase alone.
That is part of it. But I mean something bigger than that: an assurance that I am, despite imperfections, a real, positive person; that
somewhere in the sweeping, intricate pattern of people there is a
special place where I can make myself fit.

It took me years to discover and strengthen this assurance. It had
to start with the most elementary things. Once a man gave me an
indoor baseball. I thought he was mocking me and I was hurt. "I
can't use this," I said. "Take it with you," he urged me, "and roll it

around." The words stuck in my head. "Roll it around!" By rolling the ball I could hear where it went. This gave me an idea how to achieve a goal I had thought impossible: playing baseball At Philadelphia's Overbrook School for the Blind I invented a successful variation of baseball. We called it ground ball.

All my life I have set ahead of me a series of goals and then tried to reach them, one at a time. I had to learn my limitations. It was no good to try for something I knew at the start was wildly out of reach because that only invited the bitterness of failure. I would fail sometimes anyway but on the average I made progress.

I believe I made progress more readily because of a pattern of life shaped by certain values. I find it easier to live with myself if I try to be honest. I find strength in the friendship and interdependence of people. I would be blind indeed without my sighted friends. And very humbly I say that I have found purpose and comfort in a mortal's ambition toward Godliness. Perhaps a man without sight is blinded less by the importance of material things than other men are. All I know is that a belief in the existence of a higher nobility for men to strive for has been an inspiration that has helped me more than anything else to hold my life together.

ROBERT G. ALLMAN has succeeded in the triple fields of athletics, law, and sportscasting despite the fact that he is blind. As a child he attended Overbrook School for the Blind in Philadelphia, where he first started wrestling. After he entered the University of Pennsylvania, he won over fifty matches.

Mr. Allman was graduated from the University of Pennsylvania, Phi Beta Kappa. Following this, and aided by his brother, George (since few law books are printed in Braille), he studied law and was graduated from the University's Law School. A continuing interest in sports led him to become for a time a sportscaster for Station KYW.

Now a busy practicing Philadelphia attorney and insurance broker, he enjoys fishing, swimming, and golfing As president of the U S. Blind Golfers Association, he believes it a mistake for the sightless to seek consolation among themselves, and that "they should go out and rub elbows with the world."

Does Anybody Believe an Actor?

BY LIONEL BARRYMORE

FIRST OFF, I think the world has come a mighty long way toward believing that what a man does to make a living can't rob him of his integrity as a human being, when it will listen to an actor talk about what he believes. I can remember when nobody believed an actor and didn't care what he believed. Why, the very fact that he was an actor made almost everything he said open to question, because acting was thought to be a vocation embraced exclusively by scatterbrains, show-offs, wastrels and scamps. I don't believe that's true today and I don't think it ever was. I don't think there were ever any more ne'er-do-wells, rogues, poseurs and villains in the acting profession than in any other line of work. At least I hope that's the case. If it isn't, it's too late to change my mind and much too late to change my profession.

The fact is, I think, every successful man today has prepared for his success by planning and living his life in much the same way that an actor plans and creates a part. We don't make anything up out of whole cloth when we decide the way we want to play a role, any more than the author, who wrote it, made it up out of thin air. The author has one or two or perhaps a great many models in mind from which he takes a little here and a little there until he's built up a new character out of substantial material. The actor who must play this part now has to dig back into his life and recall one or two or more people who are, in some way, similar to the person the author put on paper. What I'm saying is, everybody connected with the actor's work had a model and copied this model, more or less exactly, adding to it here and there, until something new emerged. I think this is the way a person must plan his life. Adopting, borrowing and adapting a little here and a little there from his predecessors and his contemporaries, then adding a few touches until he's created himself.

I believe the difference between an eminently successful person

3

and one whose life is just mediocre is the difference between a person who had an aim, a focus, a model upon which he superimposed his own life and one who didn't. To put it bluntly, you can't get anywhere unless you know where to start from and where to go

The thing to be careful of in choosing a model is: don't aim too high for your capacity. It's necessary, it's true, to believe in the Almighty, but don't make Him your model. Have faith in Him but try for something you're more apt to make. Shoot a little closer to home. If you keep aiming at an attainable target, you can always raise your sights on another and more difficult one. But if you start off for the impossible, you're foredoomed to eternal failure.

I believe if a man remembers that, sets an attainable goal for himself and works to attain it, conscious that when he does so he will then set another goal for himself, he will have a full, busy and for this reason a happy life.

LIONEL BARRYMORE was "born to the trade." A native of Philadelphia, he was the son of Maurice and Georgianna (Drew) Barrymore His theatrical career began when he was still a child, and his formal stage debut came in 1893 when he was seen in *The Rivals* with his grandmother, Mrs. John Drew.

After appearing in other productions, he became associated with the great D. W. Griffith and the old Biograph film studio. Returning to Broadway, he acted in such plays as *The* Copperhead, *The Jest* (with Brother John), and *Macbeth.* Again attracted to the movies, he established a new reputation in the "talkies," winning an Academy Award in 1931.

Lately handicapped, he has captivated a new generation by his playing of "patriarch invalid roles." His annual radio broadcast of "A Christmas Carol," in which he plays Scrooge, has become a tradition Successful also as a composer and a writer (with a novel to his credit), he now lives on his farm in California.

How to Give Your Money Away

BY DR. SAMUEL M. BEST

MANY YEARS AGO I met a man whose unique psychology helped me to shed a life of struggle and uneasiness for great happiness, for peace of mind, and for a measure of success I otherwise would not have attained.

His name was George Robert White, a man who was orphaned and impoverished at a tender age. Yet, a man whose God-given beliefs made him both a material and a spiritual millionaire at thirty.

My path to success, and to what I had considered its natural result—happiness—was the ordinary road over which most American businessmen travel, namely, endless hours of hard work, social contacts, wise investments, headaches and heartaches.

To be sure, in a materialistic sense, I had traveled a long way from my father's farm in Nova Scotia. I had become an executive in a multi-million-dollar drug firm. But where was the resulting happiness that my material gain was supposed to have afforded me?

In my private moments of mental inventory, I discovered that I had no more peace of mind, nor was I less afraid of the problems of life and death, than many years before, when I planned my road to happiness and success by the flickering lamp in my father's tiny farmhouse. The reason was, I had neglected spiritual values in my anxiety for material gain.

It took the kindly advice of George Robert White, to open the pathway for me to happiness and freedom of mind. The important lesson Mr. White taught me is this: If we are to be happy, if we are to be successful in every aspect of the word, if we are to live truly full lives, we must share ourselves, as well as our material gain, with our fellow men.

As a young man, Mr. White took over the leadership of a small soap-manufacturing plant in Boston, and throughout his career he gave away to charity a large part of his net profits.

5

Yet, despite his unusual business practices, Mr White built that tiny concern into the world-famous Cuticura Corporation, and became the multi-million-dollar manufacturer of Cuticura Soap, Ointment and Shampoo.

I shall never forget Mr. White's words: "Personal success, business success, built upon materialism alone, are empty shells concealing disappointment, saddened lives," which he epitomized by saying: "Cast your bread upon the waters and it will come back in abundance."

Since Mr. White's death, I have endeavored, as his successor, to adhere to his code of ethics Two dollars out of every three dollars profit earned by our corporation is shared with others in helping to make our nation a better place in which to live.

We, in our corporation, believe that it is not sufficient only to manufacture as fine a product as is possible—millions of dollars over the years are being shared by our corporation for the advancement of medicine and science, for chemical research, for art and for beauty.

In my personal life I have adopted Mr. White's beliefs, and, in doing so, I have become much better equipped to serve humanity.

My reward, my blessings, have come to me in the form of personal satisfaction and peace of mind that had been substantially foreign to me.

Yes, I believe that spirituality is the needed seasoning to America's materialism. But it must be that kind of spirituality that takes the form of help and service toward our fellow men.

◄§ DR. SAMUEL M BEST IS a small-town boy who has achieved great business success and has used that success to help others Born in Maitland, Nova Scotia, he worked his way through the schools of New Hampshire and Massachusetts, graduating from the Massachusetts College of Pharmacy

Joining the Cuticura Corporation, he soon became its president. Thereafter, he devoted much time and energy to strengthening and developing the two educational institutions which had helped him on his way to success.

Today, in addition to his world-wide business responsibilities, he serves as active President of the Massachusetts College of Pharmacy. He is also Chairman of the Board of Trustees of Colby Junior College This modern, progressive school for women is an outgrowth of the small New Hampshire academy which Dr. Best once attended His love for this institution is so strong that he has built his new home just off the campus.

About Secrets and Falling Tiles

BY CARROLL BINDER

"WE ARE ALL at the mercy of a falling tile," Julius Caesar reminds us in Thornton Wilder's *Ides of March*. None of us knows at what hour something we may love may suffer some terrible blow by a force we can neither anticipate nor control.

Fifty-five years of living, much of the time in trouble centers of a highly troubled era, have not taught me how to avoid being hit by falling tiles. I have sustained some very severe blows. My mother died when I was three years old. My first-born son, a gifted and idealistic youth, was killed in the war. While I was still cherishing the hope that he might be alive, circumstances beyond my control made it impossible for me to continue work into which I had poured my heart's blood for twenty years.

I speak of such things here in the hope of helping others to believe with me that there are resources within one's grasp which enable one to sustain such blows without being crushed or embittered by them.

I believe the best hope of standing up to falling tiles is through developing a sustaining philosophy and state of mind all through life. I have seen all sorts of people sustain all sorts of blows in all sorts of circumstances by all sorts of faiths, so I believe anyone can find a faith that will serve his needs if he persists in the quest.

One of the best ways I know of fortifying oneself to withstand the vicissitudes of this insecure and unpredictable era is to school oneself to require relatively little in the way of material possessions, physical satisfactions or the praise of others. The less one requires of such things the better situated one is to stand up to changes of fortune.

I am singularly rich in friendships. Friends of all ages have contributed enormously to my happiness and helped me greatly in times of need. I learned one of the great secrets of friendship early in life—to regard each person with whom one associates as an end in himself, not a means to one's own ends. That entails trying to help those

7

with whom one comes in contact to find fulfillment in their own way while seeking one's own fulfillment in one's own way.

Another ethical principle that has stood me in good stead is: Know thyself! I try to acquaint myself realistically with my possibilities and limitations. I try to suit my aspirations to goals within my probable capacity to attain. I may have missed some undiscovered possibilities for growth but I have spared myself much by not shooting for stars it clearly was not given me to attain.

I have seen much inhumanity, cheating, corruption, sordidness and selfishness but I have not become cynical I have seen too much that is decent, kind and noble in men to lose faith in the possibility for a far finer existence than yet has been achieved. I believe the quest for a better life is the most satisfying pursuit of men and nations.

I love life but I am not worried about death. I do not feel that I have lost my son and a host of others dear to me by death. I believe with William Penn that "they that love beyond the World cannot be separated by it Death is but Crossing the World, as Friends do the Seas; they live in one another still." Death, I believe, teaches us the things of deathlessness.

CARROLL BINDER, one of America's most distinguished editors, comes of Pennsylvania Quaker stock He was completely self-supporting before he was sixteen, a cum laude graduate of Harvard at twenty Serving with a Quaker Red Cross unit in World War I, he developed a consuming urge to understand the world of people.

As foreign correspondent, then director of the foreign service of the Chicago Daily News, he covered Fascism's rise in Italy, critical phases of the Nazi and Soviet revolutions. He has traveled to nearly all parts of the world, observed international affairs with rare insight for more than a quarter of a century.

A stocky man with a thatch of straight silver-blond hair, gold-rimmed spectacles framing his steady gaze, Mr. Binder is editorial editor of the Minneapolis Tribune Besides a son killed in the war, he and his wife have another son, two daughters and four grandchildren. He has a zest for nature, swimming, the theater, good books and people.

Life in a Violin Case

BY ALEXANDER BLOCH

IN ORDER to tell what I believe, I must briefly sketch something of my personal history.

The turning point of my life was my decision to give up a promising business career and study music. My parents, although sympathetic, and sharing my love of music, disapproved of it as a profession. This was understandable in view of the family background. My grandfather had taught music for nearly forty years at Springhill College in Mobile and, though much beloved and respected in the community, earned barely enough to provide for his large family. My father often said it was only the hardheaded thriftiness of my grandmother that kept the wolf at bay. As a consequence of this example in the family, the very mention of music as a profession carried with it a picture of a precarious existence with uncertain financial rewards. My parents insisted upon college instead of a conservatory of music, and to college I went—quite happily, as I remember, for although I loved my violin and spent most of my spare time practicing, I had many other interests.

Before my graduation from Columbia, the family met with severe financial reverses and I felt it my duty to leave college and take a job. Thus was I launched upon a business career—which I always think of as the wasted years.

Now I do not for a moment mean to disparage business. My whole point is that it was not for me. I went into it for money, and aside from the satisfaction of being able to help the family, money is all I got out of it. It was not enough. I felt that life was passing me by. From being merely discontented I became acutely miserable. My one ambition was to save enough to quit and go to Europe to study music. I used to get up at dawn to practice before I left for "downtown," distracting my poor mother by bolting a hasty breakfast at the last minute. Instead of lunching with my business associates,

9

I would seek out some cheap café, order a meager meal and scribble my harmony exercises. I continued to make money, and finally, bit by bit, accumulated enough to enable me to go abroad. The family being once more solvent, and my help no longer necessary, I resigned from my position and, feeling like a man released from jail, sailed for Europe. I stayed four years, worked harder than I had ever dreamed of working before and enjoyed every minute of it.

"Enjoyed" is too mild a word. I walked on air. I really lived. I was a free man and I was doing what I loved to do and what I was meant to do

If I had stayed in business I might be a comparatively wealthy man today, but I do not believe I would have made a success of living. I would have given up all those intangibles, those inner satisfactions that money can never buy, and that are too often sacrificed when a man's primary goal is financial success.

When I broke away from business it was against the advice of practically all my friends and family. So conditioned are most of us to the association of success with money that the thought of giving up a good salary for an idea seemed little short of insane. If so, all I can say is "Gee, it's great to be crazy."

Money is a wonderful thing, but it is possible to pay too high a price for it.

◂§ ALEXANDER BLOCH is conductor of the Florida West Coast Symphony Orchestra. Before devoting himself to conducting, he had wide and varied experience in other fields of music He went to Russia to study with Leopold Auer and stayed to become concert master of a Russian symphony orchestra—probably the only American who has held such a position He has written works for the violin, composed operettas and songs, and held college and conservatory posts.

Though a rather shy man away from the podium, Mr. Bloch welcomes his devoted fellow musicians and students when they come to call. Between rehearsals and concerts in Sarasota, his home, he plays in a string quartet which he has organized with his first-desk orchestra members Summers he spends on his farm near Hillsdale, New York. He states that music is his only hobby When reminded that music is his profession, and asked again to name a hobby, he replies, "More music."

Man Is Like a Fruit Tree

BY ELMER H. BOBST

ONCE, while taking my boat down the inland waterway to Florida, I decided to tie up at Georgetown, South Carolina, for the night and visit with an old friend. As we approached the Esso dock, I saw him through my binoculars standing there awaiting us. Tall and straight as an arrow he stood, facing a cold, penetrating wind—truly a picture of a sturdy man, even though in his eighties. Yes, the man was our elder statesman, Bernard Baruch.

He loaded us into his station wagon and we were off to his famous Hobcaw Barony for dinner. We sat and talked in the great living room where many notables and statesmen, including Roosevelt and Churchill, have sat and taken their cues. In his eighty-second year, still a human dynamo, Mr. Baruch talked not of the past but of present problems and the future, deploring our ignorance of history, economics and psychology. His only reference to the past was to tell me, with the wonderful sparkle in his eye, that he was only able to get eight quail out of the ten shots the day before. What is the secret of this great man's value to the world? The answer is his insatiable desire to keep being productive.

Another friend of mine, the head of one of our largest corporations, a great steel company, is approaching his middle seventies, and he is still a great leader. He, too, never talks of the past. Instead, he tackles the problems of each day in his stride, brims with plans for the future and, incidentally, shoots in the low seventies on any golf course. He is a happy man because he is productive.

Two of the hardest things to accomplish in this world are to acquire wealth by honest effort and, having gained it, to learn how to use it properly. Recently, I walked into the locker room of a rather well-known golf club after finishing a round. It was in the late afternoon and most of the members had left for their homes. But a half dozen or so men past middle age were still seated at tables,

11

talking aimlessly and drinking more than was good for them. These same men can be found there day after day and, strangely enough each one of these men had been a man of affairs and wealth, successful in business and respected in the community. If material prosperity were the chief requisites for happiness, then each one should have been happy. Yet, it seemed to me, something very important was missing, else there would not have been the constant effort to escape the realities of life through Scotch and soda. They knew, each one of them, that their productivity had ceased. When a fruit tree ceases to bear its fruit, it is dying. And it is even so with man.

What is the answer to a long and happy existence in this world of ours? I think I found it long ago in a passage from the book of Genesis which caught my eyes while I was thumbing through my Bible. The words were few but they became indelibly impressed on my mind: "In the sweat of thy face shalt thou eat thy bread."

To me that has been a challenge from my earliest recollections. In fact, the battle of life, of existence, is a challenge to everyone. The immortal words of St. Paul, too, have been and always will be a great inspiration to me. At the end of the road I want to be able to feel that I have fought a good fight—I have finished the course—I have kept the faith.

ELMER HOLMES BOBST was born in a Lutheran parsonage in Clear Spring, Maryland. After an education which included a year at Franklin and Marshall Academy, he left home to learn pharmacy as a drug clerk Studying at night, with secondhand textbooks, he passed the state examinations. With this background, he became a representative for the then small pharmaceutical house of Hoffmann-LaRoche Company. He rose in time to be general manager, then vice-president and, later, president. Under his management the company became a leader in its field.

He retired at sixty to devote himself to his philanthropies and to enjoy some golf, fishing, and yachting. Within a year, however, he was back in business —as president of Warner-Hudnut, Inc. Mr Bobst contributes much time to the American Cancer Society, of which he is honorary chairman. As chairman of the U.S Savings Bonds Division, he represents the Treasury Department in the State of New Jersey. He lives in Montclair.

The Invisible Medicine of Humanity

BY DR. EDMUND A. BRASSET

ANY DOCTOR who is moderately active sees, in the course of a year, at least a couple of thousand people in his office. In almost eighteen years of practice I have had a good many people sit alongside my desk and tell me of their illnesses, anxieties and often personal tragedies. From this store of experience I have learned at least one basic truth, namely, that every man, woman and child on this earth, regardless of his or her station in life, regardless of racial origin, regardless even of whether he or she is moral or unmoral according to accepted standards, is worthy of and should be treated with respect, as befits the essential dignity of man.

The human body is the most ingeniously contrived mechanism and most beautiful structure on earth. Every bone is a masterpiece of architectural design. Every organ is a marvel of efficiency which no engineer can begin to equal. The smallest gland is a chemical plant that can outperform the greatest man-made laboratory in the world. If all the volumes of medical literature in the world were gathered together they would fill to overflowing the greatest of skyscrapers—and yet we have just scratched the surface of what there is to know about the human body. And over and above this complex perfection, man has something more. There is a nonmechanical and nonmaterial element in him that is not found in any other form of life that we know. We cannot see it and cannot even begin to understand it, but it is there and it raises man to a dignity above the brute.

In a small way a doctor shares the lives of a great many people. He knows their troubles, worries with them, does his best to make them well and happy and is glad with them when he succeeds. A good doctor is, within the limits of his own field, the servant of the humblest individual who needs his services. I cannot say that I have liked every single man and woman I have met—though I have liked most

13

of them—but liking has nothing to do with respect. There are people who become hypocrites, liars, thieves and murderers—just the same, they are human beings. I admit that I cannot help hating such people at times, but it doesn't last Hatred cannot last unless it is continuously nourished and stimulated.

I believe in God and that He made the earth and set it to spinning and circling around the sun. I know too that the spinning earth is not intended to turn forever. Little by little it is slowing down A day will come, perhaps a million years from now, when it will no longer turn and everything will be still. Long before that happens all the races of man will have disappeared from the face of the earth, and with him all the things he has made—his cities and roads, his machines and books But even when the last sound made by the last living creature has died away and the cold silence of eternity has settled upon this planet, I believe somehow that the spirit of man will live.

◄§ DR EDMUND A BRASSET lives with his wife and five children in Wakefield, Rhode Island Tall, friendly, and easygoing, this very human man of science has a boundless interest in the world around him

Having received his education at Danhousie University (later at Montreal and Harvard), he devoted eighteen years to a busy medical and surgical practice Although often working under difficult circumstances, he somehow found time to write his autobiography which traces his struggle from an impoverished boyhood in Nova Scotia to success as a general practitioner in Wakefield. Published as *A Doctor's Pilgrimage*, it was an immediate success

Now at work on a new book, Dr. Brasset claims that all his writing is done between the hours of four and six in the morning—the only two hours of the twenty-four, he says, that a conscientious doctor can really call his own.

Paying the Rent of Service

BY LEE HASTINGS BRISTOL

IN A COMPLEX SOCIETY and a complex civilization the individual is inevitably confused much of the time. But I believe that the basic solution of all world and group problems must first be solved by the individual himself. Each one of us, whether we publicly admit it or not, has a deeply spiritual side. Not one of us can conceal it—scratch the surface and it is always there. So first of all—and underlying all my credo—I believe in God and an orderly universe.

As a mortal, passing through this life for just a limited period of time, I believe that happiness is a truly basic objective—happiness for one's self and, hopefully, happiness for others. It hasn't taken too much living on my part to discover that *real* happiness, which sounds so selfish and self-centered, is never achieved merely by selfish materialism—it can only have depth and real satisfaction if it is bound up with unselfishness—a consideration for others. Service is the very essence of it It has been said that "service is the rent we pay for our place on earth." That kind of service brings the true happiness we all seek.

The antithesis of all this is selfishness, which is outstandingly the greatest world-wide vice. It seems as though all the world had the "gimmies," selfishly grasping for power and more power at national levels, with individuals selfishly struggling for material things at their own level.

Each one of us needs a sense of humor with its balancing factor of a sense of proportion. I believe a sense of humor brings poise and a start towards understanding.

My credo embraces a joyous approach for me towards my fellow man and for collective groups towards each other. I want none of that grim hellfire-and-brimstone stuff that flourished in the early days of our country—a religion of frightening fear of the hereafter. Why, even their old church pews were as uncomfortable as strait jackets!

A joyous approach towards living even cheers you yourself—to say nothing of its warmth that eases the burdens of others.

I believe that brotherhood can grow from this to help destroy forever the seeds of friction and injustice that stem from group minority prejudices

If only each one of us can develop a sound philosophy and work out a course of conduct as individuals, then I believe we can solve our world problems at the international level. Thomas Mann once gave this challenging definition "War is only a cowardly escape from the problems of peace." With faith and good will in our hearts and with peace in our souls and minds, surely we can leave this world the better for our having lived in it.

⋐§ LEE BRISTOL, President of Bristol-Myers Company, New York, is one of three sons of the founder of this successful pharmaceutical concern. He is a graduate of Hamilton College A tall man, he has a speaking voice and a command of language that reflect his incisive mind and sincerity.

A supporter of such organizations as the National Urban League and the National Association of Christians and Jews, Mr. Bristol in 1947 launched an Advertising Council Campaign to do away with prejudice. He thinks advertising can be used to sell not only soap and lipstick but sound ideas to strengthen racial and religious harmony.

He says his concern with furthering brotherhood grew gradually. Perhaps one reason is that he has always lived and worked in New York, a melting pot of the world. His mother also influenced him greatly When he was a child, she daily challenged him. "Lee, has your soul grown today?"

What Are People Good For?

BY INA CORINNE BROWN

ONE'S BELIEFS are revealed not so much in words or in formal creeds as in the assumptions on which one habitually acts and in the basic values by which all choices are tested.

The cornerstone of my own value system was laid in childhood by parents who believed that personal integrity came first. They never asked, "What will people think?" The question was, "What will you think of yourself if you do this or fail to do that?" Thus living up to one's own conception of oneself became a basic value and the question "What will people think?" took a subordinate place.

A second basic value, in some ways an extension of the first, I owe to an old college professor who had suffered more than his share of grief and trouble Over and over he said to us: "The one thing that really matters is to be bigger than the things that can happen to you. Nothing that can happen to you is half so important as the way in which you meet it."

Gradually I realized that here was the basis of the only real security and peace of mind that a human being can have. Nobody can be sure when disaster, disappointment, injustice or humiliation may come to him through no fault of his own. Nor can one be guaranteed against one's own mistakes and failures. But the way we meet life is ours to choose and when integrity, fortitude, dignity and compassion are our choice, the things that can happen to us lose their power over us.

The acceptance of these two basic values led to a third. If what one is and how one meets life are of first importance one is not impressed by another's money, status or power, nor does one judge people by their race, color or social position. This opens up a whole new world of relationships, for when friendships are based on qualities of mind and character one can have friends among old and young, rich and poor, famous and unknown, educated and unlettered, and among people of all races and all nations

Given these three basic values, a fourth became inevitable. It is one's duty and obligation to help create a social order in which persons are more important than things, ideas more precious than gadgets, and in which individuals are judged on the basis of personal worth. Moreover, for this judgment to be fair human beings must have an opportunity for the fullest development of which they are capable. One is thus led to work for a world of freedom and justice through those social agencies and institutions which make it possible for people everywhere to realize their highest potentialities.

Perhaps all this adds up to a belief in what has been called the human use of human beings. We are set off from the rest of the animal world by our capacity consciously to transcend our physical needs and desires Men must concern themselves with food and with other physical needs, and they must protect themselves and their own from bodily harm, but these activities are not exclusively human. Many animals concern themselves with these things. When we worship, play, or feel compassion, when we enjoy a painting, a sunset or a sonata, when we think and reason, pursue ideas, seek truth, or read a book, when we protect the weak and helpless, when we honor the noble and cherish the good, when we co-operate with our fellow men to build a better world, our behavior is worthy of our status as human beings.

§ INA CORINNE BROWN, who holds a Ph D degree from the University of Chicago, is professor of social anthropology at Scarritt College in Nashville, Tennessee She is a tall, slender, gray-haired woman who thinks anthropology one of the most exciting subjects in the world because it deals with people—all kinds of people all over the world.

Dr. Brown has done research in the British Museum and Oxford University libraries and has traveled in Europe, the West Indies, Central Africa and the Orient. She is the author of several books, including The Story of the American Negro and Race Relations in a Democracy.

She keeps house and is proud of her reputation as a cook Scarritt College welcomes students of all races and nations, and students from other countries frequently find their way not only into her classes but into her kitchen as well. There the professor turns pupil and adds new and exotic dishes to her already extensive culinary repertoire.

Friendship Is a Passport

BY JULIEN BRYAN

As a LITTLE BOY, I believed devoutly in a very personal God who listened to my every word and took a very personal interest in all of my activities. I actually talked to Him a great deal. He was a God of love, but He was also a God of fierce and rapid justice. I felt as though His eyes were on me all of the time.

I was raised a Protestant, and as I look back I can see that somewhere along the line I learned to be suspicious of and condescending to all other sects. Then, at seventeen, during the First World War, I joined the Ambulance Service of the French Army and served for six months at Verdun My friends were simple French soldiers With one or two exceptions, they were all Roman Catholics I went to Mass with them, carried them when wounded, saw them die. And I came to like them as people, to admire their courage, to respect their right to their faith which was so different from my own.

Twenty years ago, I began to make films about people all over the world. I took them as I found them—not as I wanted them to be. Wherever I went I soon discovered that when you break bread with people and share their troubles and joys, the barriers of language, of politics, and of religion soon vanish. I liked them, and they liked me. That was all that mattered.

I came to find that the peoples of this world have much more in common with one another than they have differences. I have found this true wherever I have gone—even in Moscow and the far reaches of Siberia. The most hardened Communist would eventually break down if you were kind to his children. This was true even though he knew he might be arrested the next day for becoming friendly with a foreigner.

As for the common man in Russia, my belief is that in spite of thirty-four years of Stalin and regimented thought-control, he still loves his land and his church and his family. And he hates the cruelty

19

of the secret police and the incredible stupidity of the Soviet bureaucrats In fact, I believe that in a fundamental way he is very much like us, he wants to live his own life and be let alone.

All over the world I have watched the great religions in practice—Buddhist monks at their devotions in Manchuria, Shinto priests in their temples in Japan, and only last autumn the brave and hardy Serbian Moslems at their worship in Tito's Yugoslavia I have come to hold a deep respect for all of man's great religions. And I have come to believe that despite their differences all men can worship side by side

For myself, I believe in people—and in their given right to enjoy the freedoms we so cherish in America. I believe in justice and knowledge and decent human values. I believe in each man's right to a job and food and shelter. And I sincerely believe that one day all of these things will come to pass

My real faith, then, is in a dream that in spite of daily headlines prophesying man's destruction, we can build a better world, a world of peace and human brotherhood. Yes, even in our lifetime! This is my faith and my dream. In my small way I want to have a share in making it come about.

Julien bryan has been a world traveler since he was seventeen Born in Titusville, Pennsylvania, his journeys have taken him to thirty countries. Since 1930 his time and talents have gone chiefly into exploration and the making of documentary films showing how people live in other lands. He is at present executive director of the International Film Foundation, an organization which produces documentaries to promote better international understanding.

Involved directly in both World Wars, he has written several books on his experiences, including his war diary, *Ambulance 464.* He was the last foreign correspondent to leave Warsaw in 1939 before the Germans occupied that city. The motion picture footage which he shot of those last, terrible days was incorporated in *Siege,* the first movie to be made of the Second World War.

Mr Bryan's hobbies include swimming, and cooking out of doors He lives in Bronxville, New York, with his wife and son.

Roll Away the Stone

BY PEARL BUCK

I ENJOY LIFE because I am endlessly interested in people and their growth. My interest leads me continually to widen my knowledge of people, and this in turn compels me to believe that the normal human heart is born good. That is, it is born sensitive and feeling, eager to be approved and to approve, hungry for simple happiness and the chance to live. It neither wishes to be killed nor to kill. If through circumstances it is overcome by evil, it never becomes entirely evil. There remain in it elements of good, however recessive, which continue to hold the possibility of restoration.

I believe in human beings but my faith is without sentimentality. I know that in environments of uncertainty, fear and hunger, the human being is dwarfed and shaped without his being aware of it, just as the plant struggling under a stone does not know its own condition. Only when the stone is removed can it spring up freely into the light. But the power to spring up is inherent, and only death puts an end to it.

I feel no need for any other faith than my faith in human beings. Like Confucius of old, I am so absorbed in the wonder of earth and the life upon it that I cannot think of heaven and the angels. I have enough for this life. If there is no other life, then this one has been enough to make it worth being born, myself a human being.

With so profound a faith in the human heart and its power to grow toward the light, I find here reason and cause enough for hope and confidence in the future of mankind. The common sense of people will surely prove to them someday that mutual support and co-operation are only sensible for the security and happiness of all.

Such faith keeps me continually ready and purposeful with energy to do what one person can toward shaping the environment in which the human being can grow with freedom. This environment, I believe, is based upon the necessity for security and friendship.

I take heart in the promising fact that the world contains food supplies sufficient for the entire earth population. Our knowledge of medical science is already sufficient to improve the health of the whole human race. Our resources in education, if administered on a world scale, can lift the intelligence of the race. All that remains is to discover how to administer, upon a world scale, the benefits which some of us already have. In other words, to return to my simile, the stone must be rolled away.

This, too, can be done, as a sufficient number of human beings come to have faith in themselves and in each other. Not all will have such faith at the same moment, but there is a growing number who have the faith Half a century ago no one had thought of world food, world health, world education. Many are thinking today of these things. In the midst of possible world war, of wholesale destruction, I find my only question is this Are there enough people who now believe? Is there time enough left for the wise to act? It is a contest between ignorance and death, or wisdom and life. My faith in humanity stands firm.

PEARL S. BUCK, born in the United States, lived for forty years in China. Returning to this country after having been awarded the Nobel Prize for Literature in 1938, she has launched a second career as a humanitarian which parallels that of the novelist

In such books as Of Men and Women and What America Means to Me, she has struck boldly at many major issues of our time She founded and led the East and West Movement, which works for mutual understanding among peoples.

Mrs. Buck's major interest aside from her writing is Welcome House, which she also founded Through it she finds permanent homes for homeless Asian-American children "World children" she calls them and teaches them to be proud because they have two countries, "as I myself have," she adds. Most of these children are in families near her own home, which is in Bucks County, Pennsylvania, where she lives with her husband and their four adopted children There, too, she does her writing.

Flotsam, Jetsam and Liberty

BY JAMES B. CAREY

PERHAPS MORE than anything in the world I believe in liberty. Liberty for myself, liberty for my fellow men. I can't forget the legend engraved on the base of the Statue of Liberty on Bedloe's Island in New York Harbor:

> "Give me your tired, your poor,
> Your huddled masses yearning to breathe free,
> The wretched refuse of your teeming shore.
> Send these, the homeless, tempest-lost to me;
> I lift my lamp beside the golden door "

That is the voice of America. As one small part of it, one tiny decibel in its sound, I, as a free individual of America, believe in it. It makes no boast of noble ancestry. On the contrary, it admits honestly that each of us in this country, with the possible and qualified exception of our native Indians, is a displaced person. (In a particular kind of way the Indian was our first displaced person.) If you and I did not come from abroad ourselves, our forefathers did. The scourge that drove them was economic, political or religious oppression. Oppression has always strewn the shores of life with wretched human refuse. We who today are the proud people of a proud country are what might be called the reclaimed refuse of other lands.

The fact that the flotsam and jetsam, the persecuted and the pursued of all these other lands, the fact that they came here and for the most part successfully started life anew—this renews my faith in the resilience of the human individual and the dignity of man.

There are those who say we should be content with the material benefits we have accrued among ourselves. I cannot accept that for myself A laboring man needs bread and butter, and cash to pay the rent. But he would be a poor individual indeed if he were not able to furnish the vestibule of his mind and his soul with spiritual embellishments beyond the price of a union contract.

I mean by this that I believe it is important for a man to discover, whether he is an electrical worker or an executive, that he is an individual with his own resources and a sense of the dignity of his own person and of that of other men.

We are separate, and we are collective. Man can be strong alone but not indomitable in isolation. He has to belong to something—to realize that he is not created separately or apart from the rest of mankind, whether he is an American or a Mohammedan.

I am stirred by the abundance of the fields, the forests, the streams and the natural resources they hold. But do those things make me important? Have we wrought the miracle of America because of these riches we hold? I say, "No."

Our strength—and I can say my strength too because I am a part of this whole—lies in a fundamental belief in the validity of human rights. And I believe that a man who holds these rights in proper esteem is great whether he is recognized or not.

As an individual I must face the future with honesty and faith in the good things that have made us mighty. I must have confidence in myself, in others, in all men of good will everywhere, for freedom is the child of truth and confidence.

JAMES B. CAREY is one of the country's youngest labor leaders. At twenty-five, he was president of the United Electrical and Radio Workers. When this group became affiliated with the Congress of Industrial Organizations, he was elected secretary-treasurer of the CIO, a position he still holds. Now he is president of the International Union of Electrical, Radio, and Machine Workers—CIO

Born in Philadelphia, Mr. Carey studied at Drexel Institute and the University of Pennsylvania. From his earliest days in industry he has been active in union affairs, and while holding his first job helped organize a chapter of the American Federation of Labor

Slender and athletic looking, he has served labor on various governmental committees and represented the CIO in international projects. In 1945 he was associate consultant to the United Nations Conference for Industrial Organization. He lives with his wife and two children in Silver Spring, Maryland.

Dreams Are the Stuff Life Is Made Of

BY CARROLL CARROLL

I BELIEVE I'm a very lucky man.

My entire life has been lived in the healthy area between too little and too much. I've never experienced financial or emotional insecurity, but everything I have, I've attained by my own work, not through indulgence, inheritance or privilege.

Never having lived by the abuses of any extreme, I've always felt that a workman is worthy of his hire, a merchant entitled to his profit, an artist to his reward

As a result of all this, my bargaining bump may be a little under-developed, so I've never tried to oversell myself. And though I may work for less than I know I can get, I find that because of this, I'm never so afraid of losing a job that I'm forced to compromise with my principles

Naturally in a life as mentally, physically, emotionally and finan-cially fortunate as mine has been, a great many people have helped me. A few meant to, most did so by accident. I still feel I must reciprocate. This doesn't mean that I've dedicated my life to my fellow man I'm not the type. But I do feel I should help those I'm qualified to help, just as I've been helped by others.

What I'm saying now is, I feel, part of that pattern. I think every-one should, for his own sake, try to reduce to six hundred words the beliefs by which he lives—it's not easy—and then compare those beliefs with what he enjoys—not in real estate and money and goods, but in love, health, happiness and laughter.

I don't believe we live our lives and then receive our reward or punishment in some afterlife. The life and the reward . . . the life and the punishment—these to me are one. This is my religion, coupled with the firm belief that there is a Supreme Being who planned this world and runs it so that "no man is an island, entire of himself . . ." The dishonesty of any one man subverts all honesty.

The lack of ethics anywhere adulterates the whole world's ethical content In these—honesty and ethics—are, I think, the true spiritual values.

I believe the hope for a thoroughly honest and ethical society should never be laughed at. The most idealistic dreams have repeatedly forecast the future. Most of the things we think of today as hard, practical and even indispensable were once merely dreams.

So I like to hope that the world need not be a dog-eat-dog jungle. I don't think I'm my brother's keeper. But I do think I'm obligated to be his helper. And that he has the same obligation to me.

In the last analysis, the entire pattern of my life and belief can be found in the words "Do NOT do unto others that which you would NOT have others do unto you." To say "Do unto others as you would have others DO unto you" somehow implies bargaining, an offer of favor for favor. But to restrain from acts which you, yourself, would abhor is an exercise in will power that must raise the level of human relationship.

"What is unpleasant to thyself," says Hillel, "THAT do NOT unto thy neighbor. This is the whole law," and he concluded, "All else is exposition."

CARROLL CARROLL, in charge of Hollywood operations for a large advertising agency, quit the more formal avenues of education at seventeen to "learn by doing" and got a job in advertising. Later he wrote for various New York newspapers and composed Broadway revue sketches and songs. As a contributor to all the humorous magazines that sparkled in the twenties and thirties, Mr. Carroll's wide-open grin disproves the theory that all humorists are confirmed misanthropes.

This diversified background prepared him for a career in radio and he created shows for many of the big names, including Bing Crosby, whose Music Hall he originated and wrote for over ten years This naturally led to a collaboration with Bob Hope on Hope's two famous books

With his wife and three children Mr. Carroll lives in what he calls "the happiest home in Beverly Hills."

Keep the Innocent Eye

BY SIR HUGH CASSON

WHEN I ACCEPTED the invitation to join in "This I Believe," it was not—goodness knows—because I felt I had anything profound to contribute. I regarded it—selfishly, perhaps—as a chance to get my own ideas straight. I started, because it seemed simplest that way, with my own profession The signposts I try to follow as an architect are these: to keep the innocent eye with which we are all born, and therefore always to be astonished; to respect the scholar but not the style snob, to like what I like without humbug, but also to train my eye and mind so that I can say why I like it; to use my head but not to be frightened to listen to my heart (for there are some things which can be learned only through emotion); finally, to develop to the best of my ability the best that lies within me.

But what, you may say, about the really big problems of life— Religion? Politics? World Affairs? Well, to be honest, these great problems do not weigh heavily upon my mind. I have always cared more for the small simplicities of life—family affection, loyalty of friends, joy in creative work.

Religion? Well, when challenged I describe myself as "Church of England," and as a child I went regularly to church But today, though I respect churchgoing as an act of piety and enjoy its sidelines, so to speak, the music and the architecture, it holds no significance for me. Perhaps, I don't know, it is the atmosphere of death in which religion is so steeped that has discouraged me—the graveyards, the parsonical voice, the thin damp smell of stone Even today a "holy" face conjures up not saintliness but moroseness. So, most of what I learned of Christian morality I think I really learned indirectly at home and from friends.

World Affairs? I wonder if some of you remember a famous prewar cartoon. It depicted a crocodile emerging from a peace conference and announcing to a huge flock of sheep (labeled "People of the

World"), "I am so sorry we have failed. We have been unable to restrain your warlike ambitions" Frankly, I feel at home with those sheep—mild, benevolent, rather apprehensive creatures, acting together by instinct and of course very, very woolly. But I have learned too, I think, that there is still no force, not even Christianity, so strong as patriotism; that the instinctive wisdom with which we all act in moments of crisis—that queer code of conduct which is understood by all but never formulated—is a better guide than any panel of professors; and finally that it is the inferiority complex, usually the result of an unhappy or unlucky home, which is at the bottom of nearly all our troubles. Is the solution, then, no more than to see that every child has a happy home? I'm not sure that it isn't. Children are nearer truth than we are They have the innocent eye.

If you think that such a philosophy of life is superficial or tiresomely homespun or irresponsible, I will remind you in reply that the title of this series is "This I Believe"—not "This I ought to believe," nor even "This I would like to believe"—but, "This I Believe."

§ SIR HUGH CASSON was knighted for his work as chief architect for the Festival of Britain. Now in his early forties, this slender, sharp-featured man is both a practicing architect and Reader in Interior Design at the Royal College of Art.

Having wanted to be an architect since he was eight, he went to Cambridge to study the subject. After graduating, his first assignment was to design a cashier's desk for a hairdresser's shop He was not discouraged, he says, when it was found to be too large and had to be dismantled on the street.

Sir Hugh's wife is also an architect, and they live with their three daughters in London In a recent interview he offered the following as his resolutions "To build a real building . . . To clean my shoes (nobody does except when I do, which isn't very often) . . . To be less flippant. None of these, I suspect, will be kept"

The Creed of a Soldier

BY GENERAL LUCIUS D. CLAY

IN THE MIDDLE of the war against Hitler, if somebody had told me
that I would one day be standing in the heart of Berlin before several
hundred thousand of the citizens demonstrating their desire to be
free, I would have said the person was crazy. Yet that very thing
happened to me when I returned to the former German capital
with the Freedom Bell, the symbol of the American campaign to
pierce the Iron Curtain with the propaganda of truth. In open and
dangerous defiance of the Russians and their East German puppets,
thousands of West and East Berliners gathered in the middle of the
city in a moving demonstration against tyranny. If they had believed
in tyranny a few years before, they believed in it no longer. They had
seen what democracy could mean and they wanted it.

I cite this incident to support my conviction that, given the proper
circumstances, and some hope, man as an individual, wherever he
may live, will demonstrate that he is inherently honest and decent.
He wants little more than to live in friendship with his neighbor, in
reasonable security, and to raise his children so they may find opportunity before them.

I think the troubled world in which we live should not dismay us.
I believe the world today is historically a better world than the world
of the past. Though ruthless men still maintain power through force
and would extend power through conquest, people everywhere are
becoming more tolerant and understanding than ever before. More
peoples and more governments are willing to co-operate, to work
together for peace and freedom, than at any time in history. At home
we are more tolerant and understanding with each other, more willing to help our less fortunate neighbor here and abroad.

This, to me, is hopeful progress. It stems, I think, from the spread
of freedom in which I believe and which I hold God gave us as a
privilege. Like all precious possessions, freedom must be guarded

carefully. I ask myself how I can best help guard it and the answer I find is citizenship In my view, to be a good citizen does not require the holding of public office, the achievement of either political or financial success. But it does require that I vote from conviction, that I participate in community activities to the extent that I am able, that I be honest with myself and with others.

God has been good to us as a people. As I see it, we can return thanks for the position of leadership which we now hold in world affairs, only as we exercise this leadership to obtain freedom and peace. We can lead abroad only as we continue to improve our life at home, to become truly a land in which there is equal opportunity for all. This brings me back to the personal responsibility of the individual. I believe I can improve my life here and, perhaps, help others, only as I show pride in my country by finding the time to try to be a good citizen, and by being grateful to God for His goodness.

⟡§ GENERAL LUCIUS D CLAY was graduated from the United States Military Academy in 1918 and was commissioned a Second Lieutenant in the Corps of Engineers. His first years in the service were spent mainly in construction projects, except for a period in 1937 when he served on General MacArthur's staff in the Philippines

During World War II, General Clay was Director of Matériel for the Army and then Deputy Director for War Mobilization and Reconversion. After the war he became Deputy Military Governor of the United States zone of Germany under General Eisenhower Later he held the posts of Commander-in-Chief of the United States forces in Europe and United States Military Governor of Germany. One of his accomplishments was the supervision of the gigantic air-lift operation into Berlin.

He has been awarded the Distinguished Service Medal three times, the Legion of Merit, and the Bronze Star, in addition to numerous foreign decorations. In 1950 he became Chairman of the Board of the Continental Can Company.

Causes Are People

BY SUSAN COBBS

It has not been easy for me to meet this assignment. In the first place, I am not a very articulate person, and then one has so many beliefs, changing and fragmented and transitory beliefs—besides the ones most central to our lives. I have tried hard to pull out and put into words my most central beliefs. I hope that what I say won't sound either too simple or too pious.

I know that it is my deep and fixed conviction that man has within him the force of good and the power to translate that force into life For me, this means a pattern of life that makes personal relationships more important A pattern that makes more beautiful and attractive the personal virtues: courage, humility, selflessness and love. I used to smile at my mother because the tears came so readily to her eyes when she heard or read of some incident that called out these virtues. 1 don't smile any more because I find I have become more and more responsive in the same inconvenient way to the same kind of story.

And so I believe that I both can and must work to achieve the good that is in me. The words of Socrates keep coming back to me: "The unexamined life is not worth living" By examination we can discover what is our good, and we can realize that knowledge of good means its achievement. I know that such self-examination has never been easy—Plato maintained that it was the soul's eternal search. It seems to me peculiarly difficult now. In a period of such rapid material expansion and such widespread conflicts, black and white have become gray and will not easily separate.

There is a belief which follows from this. If I have the potential of the good life within me and the compulsion to express it, then it is a power and compulsion common to all men. What I must have for myself to conduct my search, all men must have: freedom of choice, faith in the power and the beneficent qualities of truth. What frightens me most today is the denial of these rights, because this can only come from the denial of what seems to me the essential nature of man For if my conviction holds, man is more important than anything he has created and our great task is to bring back again into a subordinate position the monstrous superstructures of our society

I hope this way of reducing our problems to the human equation is not simply an evasion of them. I don't believe it is For most of us it is the only area in which we can work· the human area—with ourselves, with the people we touch, and through these two by vicarious understanding, with mankind. I believe this is the safest starting point I watch young people these days wrestling with our mighty problems. They are much more concerned with them and involved in them than my generation of students ever was They are deeply aware of the words "equality" and "justice." In their great desire to right wrong they are prone to forget that causes are people, that nothing matters more than people. They need to add to their crusades the warmer and more affecting virtues of compassion and love. And here again come those personal virtues that bring tears to the eyes.

One further word. I believe that the power of good within us is real and comes there from a source outside and beyond ourselves. Otherwise, I could not put my trust so firmly in it.

◄§ SUSAN PARKER COBBS, born in Anniston, Alabama, is a teacher of classics and a Dean of Swarthmore College. She holds degrees from Randolph-Macon Woman's College, New York University, and the University of Chicago. For twenty-five years she has taught Latin and Greek in schools and colleges, for the most part in the South, and finds in their study her deepest satisfaction. Her teaching is now an avocation, being limited to one class in beginning Greek, but she considers it one of her greatest pleasures

Though she has been at Swarthmore for seven years, her Southern accent is still noticeable. For recreation she enjoys any game or puzzle, her particular favorites being bridge, crossword puzzles, and mystery stories, "preferably not of the hard-boiled variety" Her summers are usually spent in the Adirondacks, where a mildly arduous mountain climb and the rewards of the mountaintop, she says, offer help in solving the many problems that confront her throughout the college year.

A Game of Cards

BY NORMAN COUSINS

EVER SINCE I was old enough to read books on philosophy, I have been intrigued by the discussions on the nature of man. The philosophers have been debating for years about whether man is primarily good or primarily evil, whether he is primarily altruistic or selfish, co-operative or competitive, gregarious or self-centered, whether he enjoys free will or whether everything is predetermined.

As far back as the Socratic dialogues in Plato, and even before that, man has been baffled about himself. He knows he is capable of great and noble deeds, but then he is oppressed with the evidence of great wrongdoing.

And so he wonders. I don't presume to be able to resolve the contradictions. In fact, I don't think we have to. It seems to me that the debate over good and evil in man, over free will and determinism, and over all the other contradictions—that this debate is a futile one. For man is a creature of dualism. He is both good and evil, both altruistic and selfish. He enjoys free will to the extent that he can make decisions in life, but he can't change his chemistry or his relatives or his physical endowments—all of which were determined for him at birth. And rather than speculate over which side of him is dominant, he might do well to consider what the contradictions and circumstances are that tend to bring out the good or evil, that enable him to be nobler and a responsible member of the human race. And so far as free will and determinism are concerned, something I heard in India on a recent visit to the subcontinent may be worth passing along. Free will and determinism, I was told, are like a game of cards. The hand that is dealt you represents determinism. The way you play your hand represents free will.

Now where does all this leave us? It seems to me that we ought to attempt to bring about and safeguard those conditions that tend to develop the best in man. We know, for example, that the exist-

33

ence of fear and man's inability to cope with fear bring about the worst in him. We know that what is true of man on a small scale can be true of society on a large scale. And today the conditions of fear in the world are, I'm afraid, affecting men everywhere. More than twenty-three hundred years ago, the Greek world, which had attained tremendous heights of creative intelligence and achievement, disintegrated under the pressure of fear. Today, too, if I have read the signs correctly in traveling around the world, there is great fear. There is fear that the human race has exhausted its margin for error and that we are sliding into another great conflict that will cancel out thousands of years of human progress. And people are fearful because they don't want to lose the things that are more important than peace itself—moral, democratic, and spiritual values.

The problem confronting us today is far more serious than the destiny of any political system or even of any nation. The problem is the destiny of man: first, whether we can make this planet safe for man; second, whether we can make it fit for him. This I believe— that man today has all the resources to shatter his fears and go on to the greatest golden age in history, an age which will provide the conditions for human growth and for the development of the good that resides within man, whether in his individual or his collective being. And he has only to mobilize his rational intelligence and his conscience to put these resources to work.

◄§ NORMAN COUSINS is a man of letters who has always wanted to be a baseball player. He continued to play the game for years after graduating from Teachers College, Columbia University.

He began writing on the New York Post, shifted to Current History Magazine and, later, the New York Evening Post. The Saturday Review of Literature—now the Saturday Review— next attracted him and in 1940 he became its editor, as he is today.

His books include The Good Inheritance, a history of the Athenian democracy; A Treasury of Democracy, a collection of aphorisms of freedom; and The Poetry of Freedom, an anthology on which he collaborated with the late William Rose Benét.

His dominant concern now is world federal government. He is president of the United World Federalists. He is married and has four daughters His hobby. playing and repairing his eighty-year-old Beatty church organ.

A Straight Wall Is Hard to Build

by LOU R. CRANDALL

As I TRY to outline my thoughts, the subject becomes more and more difficult. I have many basic beliefs but as I try to pick and choose it seems to me that they all can be summarized in the word "character." Obviously, what you believe is a fundamental thing. There can be no fanfare, no embellishments. It must be honest

An architect once told me that the most difficult structure to design was a simple monumental shaft. The proportions must be perfect to be pleasing The hardest thing to build is a plain straight wall. The dimensions must be absolute. In either case there is no ornamentation to hide irregularities, no moldings to cover hidden defects and no supports to strengthen concealed weaknesses.

I am using this example to illustrate human character, which to me is the most important single power in the world today. The young people of today are in reality foundations of structures yet to be built. It is obvious that the design of these human structures is the combined efforts of many human architects. Boys and girls are influenced first by their parents, then by their friends and finally by business associates. During this period of construction, the human character is revised and changed until at maturity a fairly well-fixed form of character is found

There are few human straight walls and fewer human monumental shafts. Such men and women are personalities of great beauty and are so rare that history records their being and holds them up as examples for the future. The Biblical characters are for me the closest examples of human perfection. They were unselfish, steadfast in their faith and unstinting in their help to others

Today in this world of turmoil and trouble we could use more of such people, but they do not just happen along. I believe that they are the result of concentrated effort on the part of parents and associates, and the more we build with character the better the world will become. This may sound like a dreamer's hope and a theoretical goal which can never be reached. I do not think so.

The world as a whole has progressed tremendously material-wise, and we are a fortunate nation in that we are leading the procession. It is, I believe, natural that nations not so fortunate should look upon us with envy. We would do the same if the positions were reversed, so we should not judge too harshly the efforts of others to equal our standard of living In either case, the fortunate or the unfortunate character in the individual and collectively in a nation stands out. I agree that it is easier to build character under ideal conditions but cannot forget that character is also required to give as well as receive.

It should be to the benefit of humanity if all individuals—and this includes myself—did a renovating or remodeling job on our own character. It may merely be a case of removing rough edges or tossing away molding to expose irregularities, in some cases to remove a prop and stand on one's own feet. In any event if some of us set examples, others will follow and the result should be good. This I believe.

Lou R. CRANDALL, president of the engineering firm of George A Fuller, was born in Sylvania, Ohio A graduate of Michigan, having earned a B S in Civil Engineering, he has also been awarded an honorary D Sc. from Duquesne.

Mr Crandall was a "landlocked sailor" during the First World War, serving with the Navy on shore duty in France. During the Second World War he was in charge of construction of naval bases in Quonset, Rhode Island, Newfoundland, Iceland, Northern Ireland and Scotland. He was associate executive with the Naval Procurement Program for the Seabees.

Many buildings, now landmarks in this country, were constructed under his direction, including the Supreme Court Building in Washington, the Arlington Memorial, the United Nations Building, Lever House in New York and Philadelphia's Art Museum.

Active in many charitable organizations, he has been chairman of Red Cross, New York Cancer Association, and Salvation Army campaigns.

Freedom Is Worth the Risk

BY ELMER DAVIS

THE PHILOSOPHER George Santayana, at the age of eighty-eight, admitted that things no longer seemed so simple to him as they did fifty years ago. Even those of us who have not reached Mr Santayana's age must share that feeling; but we must act by the best light we have, hoping that the light will grow brighter—and we have reason to hope it will, so long as men remain free to think. The most important thing in the world, I believe, is the freedom of the mind. All progress, and all other freedoms, spring from that. It is a dangerous freedom, but this is a dangerous world. You cannot think right without running the risk of thinking wrong; but for any evils that may come from thinking, the cure is more thinking. Over much of the world, at present, the freedom of the mind is suppressed We have got to preserve it here, despite the efforts of very earnest men to suppress it—men who say, and perhaps believe, that they are actuated by patriotism, but who are doing their best to destroy the liberties which above all are what the United States of America has meant, to its people and to humanity.

This is perhaps a less personal statement than most of those in "This I Believe" If so, it is because a man of my age, in his relation to himself, runs mostly on momentum; and it is a little difficult to look back and figure out what gave him the push, or the various pushes. What he has to consider now is what he can contribute to the present, or the future, as a member of a very peculiar species—possibly even a unique species—which has immense capacities for both good and evil, as it has amply demonstrated during its recorded history. That history to date is—barring some unpredictable cosmic disaster—the barest beginning of what may lie ahead of us. But we happen to live in one of the turning points of history—by no means the first, as it will not be the last; and the future of mankind will be more than usually affected by what we do in this generation.

What should we do? Well, first of all and above all, preserve freedom, and extend it if we can. Beyond that I don't know how better to define our business than to say we should try to promote an increase of decency. Decency in the sense of respect for other people; of taking no advantage; of never saying, "This man must be miserable in order that I may be comfortable." This is not as easy as it looks, it's impossible to exist without hurting somebody, however unintentionally. But there are limits I do not believe that human life is accurately represented by Viggeland's famous sculptured column in Oslo, of people climbing over one another and trampling one another down. The Nazis, when they occupied Norway, greatly admired that sculpture. They would. But the rest of us can do better than that; many men and women in every age have done better, and are doing it still.

The Scottish scientist J. B. S. Haldane once said that the people who can make a positive contribution to human progress are few; that most of us have to be satisfied with merely staving off the inroads of chaos. That is a hard enough job—especially in these times, when those inroads are more threatening than they have been for a long time past. But if we can stave them off, and keep the field clear for the creative intelligence, we can feel that we have done our part toward helping the human race get ahead

ELMER DAVIS, Washington news analyst for the American Broadcasting Company, once said the business of a radio commentator is a job of adult education Three Peabody awards attest only in part to his accomplishments in this field His honest explanations of the news, delivered with his characteristic Hoosier twang and wit, are known and respected by millions.

Mr. Davis was born and raised in Aurora, Ind He went to Franklin College, was a Rhodes Scholar at Oxford. Starting as a reporter on the New York Times, he has written numerous essays, short stories and half a dozen novels

His radio career began as a news analyst for CBS. From 1942 to the end of the war he directed the Office of War Information Besides integrity, his trademark is a black bow tie A leisure-loving man with snowy hair now, he is fond of bridge, travel, Latin, and symphonic music.

What Makes Me Feel Big

BY J. FRANK DOBIE

"My MIND is big when I look at you and talk to you," Chief Eagle of the Pawnees said to George Bird Grinnell when, after years of absence, that noble writer appeared at his friend's tepee

It is very difficult in drawing up a credo to be severely honest about one's self, avoiding all traditional cant We actually believe in what we value most Outside of the realms of carnality and property, which men appearing in public generally pretend not to notice, I believe in and draw nourishment from whatever makes me "feel big."

I believe in a Supreme Power, unknowable and impersonal, whose handiwork the soul-enlarging firmament declares. However, I believe in questionings, doubtings, searchings, skepticism, and I discredit credulity, or blind faith. The progress of man is based on disbelief of the commonly accepted. The noblest minds and natures of human history have thought and sung, lived and died, trying to budge the *status quo* towards a larger and fuller status. I am sustained by a belief in evolution—the "increasing purpose" of life in which the rational is with geological slowness evolving out of the irrational. To believe that goodness and wisdom and righteousness in Garden of Eden perfection lie somewhere far ahead instead of farther and farther behind gives me hope and somewhat explains existence. This is a long view I do not pretend that it is always present in me. It does raise me when I have it, however.

I feel no resentment so strongly as that against forces which make men and women afraid to speak out forthrightly. The noblest satisfaction I have is in witnessing the up movement of suppressed individuals and people. I make no pretense to having rid myself of all prejudices, but at times when I have discovered myself freed from certain prejudices, I have felt rare exhilaration.

For me the beautiful resides in the physical, but it is spiritual. I

39

have never heard a sermon as spiritual in either phrase or fact as—

"Waters on a starry night are beautiful and free."

No hymn lifts my heart higher than the morning call of the bob-white or the long fluting cry of sandhill cranes out of the sky at dusk. I have never smelled incense in a church as refining to the spirit as a spring breeze laden with aroma from a field of bluebonnets. Not all hard truths are beautiful, but "beauty is truth." It incorporates love and is incorporated by love. It is the goal of all great art. Its presence everywhere makes it free to all. It is not so abstract as justice, but beauty and intellectual freedom and justice, all incorporating truth and goodness, are constant sustainers to my mind and spirit.

J FRANK DOBIE, of Austin, Texas, calls himself "both a man and a country man." A great love of English poetry made him a teacher of English and is reflected in his book, A Texan in England, written while he was a visiting professor of American History at Cambridge University during the war.

Born and raised on a ranch in the border country of Texas, he has reverted to ranching more than once during his career as professor of English at the University of Texas. Mexi-can vaqueros, old-time trail drivers, and hunters of lost mines are some of the characters who people his many books on the Southwest, which include Coronado's Children, Apache Gold and Yaqui Silver, and The Voice of the Coyote He is also author of Guide to Life and Literature of the Southwest, and, most recently, The Mustangs

A man who is willing to take action to support his beliefs, he regards intellectual freedom as the most essential element in the free enterprise system.

I Don't Play to the Grandstand

BY BOBBY DOERR

IT SEEMS to me that what any man's beliefs are depends upon how he spends his life. I've spent a good part of mine as a professional baseball player and the game that I play for a living is naturally a very important thing to me. I've learned a lot of things on the baseball diamond about living—things that have made me happier and, I hope, a better person I've found that when I make a good play and take my pitcher off the hook, it's just natural for me to feel better than if I made a flashy play that doesn't do anything except make me look good for the grandstands. It works the same way off the ball field, too Doing a good turn for a neighbor, a friend, or even a stranger gives me much more satisfaction than doing something that helps only myself It's as if all people were my teammates in this world and things that make me closer to them are good, and things that make me draw away from them are bad.

Another belief very important to me is that I am only as good as my actual performance proves that I am If I cannot deliver, then my name and reputation don't mean a thing. I thought of this when in the spring of 1951 I told my team that I would not play in 1952. I reached this decision because I realized that I wouldn't be able to give my best performance to the people who would pay my salary by coming through the turnstiles. I don't see how anyone can feel right about success or fame that is unearned. For me, most of the satisfaction in any praise I receive comes from the feeling that it is the reward for a real effort I have made.

Many ball players talk a lot about luck and figure that it is responsible for their successes and failures, on and off the field. Some of them even carry around a rabbit's foot and other good-luck charms or they have little rituals that they go through to make sure of things going the way they want them to. I've never been able to go along with people who believe that way. I've got a feeling that there's some-

41

thing much deeper and more important behind the things that happen to me and whether they turn out good or bad. It seems to me that many of the things which some people credit to luck are the results of divine assistance. I can't imagine an all-wise, all-powerful God that isn't interested in the things I do in my life. Believing this makes me always want to act in such a way as to deserve the things that the Lord will do for me.

Maybe that's the most important thing of all. Doing good in order to deserve good. A lot of wonderful things have happened to me in my lifetime. I've had a long, rewarding career in organized baseball. The fans have been swell to me and I've always liked my teammates. But what really matters is that I've got just about the best folks that anyone could ask for. Doing what I can to make things more pleasant for my father and mother and for my wife and our son has been one of the things I have enjoyed most because it seems to be a way for me to pay back something of what I owe them for all the encouragement and pleasure they've given me.

I guess the best way to sum it all up is that I'm happy to be around and I'd like to be able to make other people glad of it, too.

ROBERT "BOBBIE" DOERR was a member of that vast army of young American boys who, when they are not actually playing the game, are dreaming about baseball His father, a baseball player himself, bought him his first pair of "spikes" when he was ten. Six years later "Bobbie" was playing second base with a Pacific Coast League team.

In 1937 he was signed to play with the Boston Red Sox of the American League. This was the team that boasted such players as Joe Cronin, Jimmy Foxx, and "Lefty" Grove, and as "Bobbie" expressed it, "It just didn't seem possible that I could be playing with them" But he did, and well enough to place him on nine All-Star teams and in a World Series.

Retired now after fifteen seasons of baseball, he lives with his wife on a 160-acre ranch near Agness, Oregon, and sends his son to the one-room schoolhouse where Mrs Doerr once taught.

My Father's Evening Star

BY WILLIAM O. DOUGLAS

DURING MOMENTS of sadness or frustration, I often think of a family scene years ago in the town of Yakima, Washington. I was about seven or eight years old at the time. Father had died a few years earlier. Mother was sitting in the living room talking to me, telling me what a wonderful man Father was. She told me of his last illness and death. She told me of his departure from Cleveland, Washington, to Portland, Oregon . . . for what proved to be a fatal operation. His last words to her were these: "If I die it will be glory, if I live it will be grace." I remember how those words puzzled me I could not understand why it would be glory to die. It would be glory to live, that I could understand. But why it would be glory to die was something I did not understand until later.

Then one day in a moment of great crisis I came to understand the words of my father "If I die it will be glory, if I live it will be grace." That was his evening star. The faith in a power greater than man. That was the faith of our fathers. A belief in a God who controlled man in the universe, that manifested itself in different ways to different people. It was written by scholars and learned men in dozens of different creeds. But riding high above all secular controversies was a faith in One who was the Creator, the Giver of Life, the Omnipotent.

Man's age-long effort has been to be free. Throughout time he has struggled against some form of tyranny that would enslave his mind or his body. So far in this century, three epidemics of it have been let loose in the world.

We can keep our freedom through the increasing crisis of history only if we are self-reliant enough to be free—dollars, guns, and all the wondrous products of science and the machine will not be enough. "This night thy soul shall be required of thee."

These days I see graft and corruption reach high into government.

43

These days I see people afraid to speak their minds because someone will think they are unorthodox and therefore disloyal. These days I see America identified more and more with material things, less and less with spiritual standards. These days I see America drifting from the Christian faith, acting abroad as an arrogant, selfish, greedy nation, interested only in guns and in dollars . . . not in people and their hopes and aspirations. These days the words of my father come back to me more and more. We need his faith, the faith of our fathers. We need a faith that dedicates us to something bigger and more important than ourselves or our possessions. Only if we have that faith will we be able to guide the destiny of nations, in this the most critical period of world history.

WILLIAM ORVILLE DOUGLAS, Associate Justice of the United States Supreme Court, is a warm, friendly man who believes in what he calls "bedrock idealism." Just under six feet tall, with sandy, tousled hair, he does not present the usual conception of the learned judge which he indubitably is. The truth is, Mr. Justice Douglas is equally at home in our highest court and in the saddle of a spirited horse. He spends his summers on adventurous trips to remote lands.

He is a graduate of Whitman College and of Columbia University Law School Later he taught law both at Columbia and at Yale. Robert M. Hutchins has called him "the outstanding professor of law in the nation " He became chairman of the Securities Exchange Commission in 1937. Franklin D Roosevelt appointed him to the Supreme Court in 1939 to succeed the late great Louis Brandeis. He is a man of simple honesty with a fierce belief in democracy.

White Is Made of Many Colors

CAROLINE DUER

I AM CONVINCED that any religion in which a man is good—and un-bigoted—is a good religion for him and should be held in esteem. Just as white is made up of many colors, so every section in the whole of it is many-tinted. This is true of faiths.

To "know thyself" seems to me truly the beginning of wisdom, and one cannot start the study too early. I believe in fastidious honesty toward others, and I would try to demand the same of myself to myself. I believe in justice, generosity and kindness.

To cultivate a sense of proportion, a sense of humor, is a great help in daily life. The "put yourself in his place" attitude, even if, later, you find you are obliged to knock "him" out of it, is an admirable attitude. I forget which of our great generals said, "Let the other man tell his story first"; but it is a good principle—a part of that wisdom and understanding which helps to keep the world going round even in the rather wobbly way it is going.

I believe in courage, in facing whatever has to be faced and taking pride in so doing.

I believe in patience; in politeness; in reason and routine—reason in the laying out of my day, routine in following my own rules and in doing whatever is to be done as well as I can do it.

Perhaps I can sum up my beliefs most clearly by quoting a verse of mine which is really more grave in intent than it may appear at first sight. I call it "Advice, Gratuitous, About Living."

> Collect the most agreeable thoughts and think them,
>   But face the least agreeable without dread.
> Esteem good foods, good wines, and eat and drink them
>   In company, or with a book instead.
> Dress, though alone, as well as you are able;
> It seems to make the meal more palatable.

45

Be reasonable and courteous in commanding;
   Show kindness, it comes back a thousandfold.
Tutor your heart to wisdom's understanding
   And none shall note if it be warm or cold.
Dare to ask Fate for life's supremest portion
And be not prisoner to your own precaution.

What time your work-days in the world are over,
   Find pleasant tasks for head and hand at home.
The chances are that you may yet discover
   Some hidden talent for the years to come.
But shirk no obligations, though they daunt you,
These are things that may return to haunt you.

Fear little, and you'll little have for fearing.
   Regret is wasted in the Master-plan.
Bear what you must and profit by the bearing.
   Respect all creeds; believe in what you can.
And on your own mishaps spend not much sorrow.
The day is dark: It may be fair tomorrow.

CAROLINE DUER, poet, was born in late February of the year that President Lincoln was shot. She has always felt particularly at home with older people, which she attributes to the fact that, as her sisters were so much younger, she was dependent upon her mother and father, uncles and aunts, for her amusement, early education, and companionship. She is a New Yorker.

She has always been fond of solitary pastimes such as sewing, painting, music and reading. She began to write at an early age, and although she says "my verse was better than my prose," the magazines have always welcomed both.

Long interested in hospital work, Miss Duer spent long periods in France during the First World War. Returning to this country in 1920, she joined the staff of Vogue, remaining there for eleven years. Nowadays, she declares, she finds the ancient art of découpage, a sort of paper marquetry, a pleasantly satisfying hobby.

A Lesson Learned at Midnight

BY JAMES Q. DU PONT

EVER SINCE one midnight, in nineteen hundred and nine—when I first heard my mother crying—I have been groping for beliefs to help me through the rough going and confusions of life My dad's voice was low and troubled as he tried to comfort Mother—and in their anguish they both forgot the nearness of my bedroom. I overheard them. I was only seven then, and while their problem of that time has long since been solved and forgotten, the big discovery I made that night *is still* right with me—life is *not* all hearts and flowers. It's hard and cruel for most of us much of the time. We *all* have troubles—they just differ in nature, that's all. And that leads to my first belief.

I believe the human race is very, very tough—almost impossible to discourage. If it wasn't, then why do we have such words as "laugh" and "sing" and "music" and "dance"—in the language of all mankind since the beginning of recorded time? This belief makes me downright proud to be a human being.

Next, I believe there is *good and evil* in all of us. Thomas Mann comes close to expressing what I'm trying to say with his carefully worded sentence about the "frightfully radical duality" between the brain and the beast in man—in all of us.

This belief helps me because so long as I remember that there are certain forces of evil ever present in me—and never forget that there is also a divine spark of goodness in me, too—then I find that the "score" of my bad mistakes and regrets at the end of each day is greatly reduced. "Forewarned of evil is half the battle against it."

I believe in trying to be charitable, in trying to understand and forgive people, especially in trying to forgive very keen or brilliant people. A man may be a genius but he can still do things that practically break your heart

I believe most if not *all* of our very finest thoughts and many of

47

our finest deeds must be kept to ourselves alone—at least until after we die. This used to confuse me. But now I realize that by their very nature, these finest things we do and cannot talk about are a sort of secret preview of a better life to come.

I believe there is no escape from the rule that we must do many, many little things to accomplish even just one big thing. This gives me patience when I need it most

And then I believe in having the courage to BE MYSELF. Or perhaps I should say, to be honest with myself. Sometimes this is practically impossible, but I'm sure I should always try.

Finally, and most important to me, I do believe in God. I'm sure there is a very wise and wonderful Being who designed, constructed and operates this existence as we mortals know it. this universe with its galaxies and spiral nebulae, its stars and moons and planets and beautiful women, its trees and pearls and deep green moss—and its hopes and prayers for peace.

JAMES Q DU PONT, of the Du Pont Company's Public Relations Department, might seem to have wandered far afield from his M.I.T. engineering training Actually, as friends point out, his experience as engineer, industrial photographer and speaker have combined to give him an excellent background for his work

Slender, intense, and with a warm and understanding smile, Mr. du Pont has been associated with the Du Pont Company since 1940. His work has included construction and engineering jobs on a cellophane plant at Clinton, Iowa, and assignments with the early atomic energy program at the University of Chicago and Oak Ridge, Tennessee.

Mr du Pont is a native of Johnstown, Pennsylvania He is married and now lives, with his wife and four children, close by the old site where his great-great-grandfather established the Du Pont Company in 1802. He has reached nation-wide audiences with his talent for explaining complex subjects in down-to-earth terms.

What Does God Say to Me?

BY DAME EDITH EVANS

I BELIEVE that good is stronger than evil. I have found that if applied with complete faith, it can obliterate evil.

Knowledge like this gives one great strength in times of oppression or tyranny. I believe that hatred is destructive. It is not always easy, or possible, to love people, nations, or ideas but at least, I say to myself, "Do not hate them· try to turn thoughts toward God." Someone once said. "It is better to love the good than hate the bad "

I have all of my share of the artist's temperament, and one of our faults is that we think people are being unfair to us, or that we are suffering from other people's jealousy. The persecution complex, in fact. The one and only way in which I have been able to clear this away is to turn my mind and thought to good and to God. I say: "Never mind what he or she or they say, what does God say to me? Where does my life come from? Who is the source of all my qualities —and can anything prevent those qualities from being used?"

I believe today that a great flood of good would be released in the world if all of us concentrated upon following the simple commands of Christ: "Love God first and your neighbor as yourself." As "yourself" I try to remember. So if I think kindly of myself then I think kindly of my neighbor. When Christ was asked, "Who is my neighbor?" what did He say? He told the story of the Samaritan.

People are always demanding of us British. "Don't you dislike Americans?" And conversely to you Americans: "Don't you dislike the British?" I can't bear classing people together nationally, and liking or disliking them. People are people wherever you meet them. They are all the children of the one God.

I have been asked how I felt in the Blitz. Most of the time I was in London—terribly excited by fear. But the only way I could keep going about my work at all was by constantly assuring myself that the all-powerful God would take care of me.

On looking round the everyday world today, one is impressed by the amount of fear that is expressed by everybody Fear of war, fear of ill health, fear of not being able to hold their job, fear of people getting in before them, fear of losing opportunity. Fear of losing friends, lovers, advantages. Fear of death.

We are constantly reading articles, and hearing speeches, where the writers and the speakers tell us that we must cease being so material But what most of us want to know is, How. If a busy man at his office is faced with a seemingly insuperable problem, how is he to solve this problem by other than material means? But of course the answer is so simple. Like Naaman who said: "Are not Abana and Pharpar, rivers of Damascus, better than all the waters of Israel?" we tend to disregard it. It is always to turn our thoughts immediately, and with absolute confidence, away from the difficulty, and if, as I said at the beginning, one believes in the power of good, one must quietly know that the power of good will give the right answer to the problem, even if the answer is required within a few minutes or half an hour.

And when I say these things, I say them because I have proved them. In fact, throughout the ups and downs of my theatrical life, if I had not had some simple code, because I am not a highly intellectual woman, I should not be doing happily and successfully the work that I love.

◄§ DAME EDITH EVANS holds honorary degrees from London University and Cambridge, the first actress to be so honored. Her achievements fill four columns in the British Who's Who in the Theatre She was the first West End actress to go to the Old Vic, and she created four Bernard Shaw roles— the Serpent and the She-Ancient in Back to Methuselah, Lady Utterwood in Heartbreak House, Orinthia in The Apple Cart, and Epifania in The Millionairess. During the war she traveled extensively to entertain the troops.

American audiences first saw her on Broadway in 1931 as Florence Nightingale in The Lady With a Lamp. They will long remember her as the Nurse to Katharine Cornell's Juliet. She has appeared too in films

Although Dame Edith has always called London her home, she has a great love of the English countryside and still maintains a home in Kent Walking, boating, and driving are among this distinguished lady's hobbies.

Spiritual Handholds on Life

BY DR. FRED DOW FAGG, JR.

THE VIEW of the high Sierra Lake, nestled in the snow and rock slightly below the timber line, was beautiful from my vantage point some five hundred feet above its shimmering surface. I was anxious to rejoin my companions and try the fishing before the afternoon shadows—edging out from the surrounding array of peaks—entirely covered the lake. Just a short distance beyond the intervening shale, the trail zigzagged down to the valley. I disliked the thought of returning by the long, tedious trail I had ascended, and decided to chance the shale—even though part of it lay above a sheer drop-off of several hundred feet.

I started working my way over the loose rock with considerable caution and had covered about half the distance when I became aware of a slight but persistent yielding of the shale under my feet. Desperately, I looked for something that would offer support and lurched forward to grasp a light outcropping of solid rock just as the surface shale underfoot—loosened from its foundation by the warm noonday sun—cascaded downward and disappeared over the cliff. Several seconds passed before I heard it rattle into the lake.

Finally—after due consideration of the folly of short cuts—I managed to move from handhold to handhold and, at last, pulled myself to the trail by the aid of a dwarf juniper root. I have forgotten how many trout I caught that afternoon, but I have not forgotten the value of a handhold.

Handholds are needed also during the course of everyday life. They provide security when the things we depend upon seem to be slipping out from under us. What are the spiritual handholds I have found to be of most value?

First, the teachings of the humble carpenter of Nazareth—for their insistence on the supreme worth of the individual, for their stressing

51

of the significance of sympathetic understanding, and for their unsurpassed evidence of dauntless faith.

Second, the conviction that, while every person should delight in making a courageous and self-reliant effort to live up to his capabilities, there are well-springs of power outside himself that can be tapped—if he will avail himself of them.

Third, that the nature of this world and of the people in it is determined more by our individual vision, understanding and conduct than by any material environmental factors, and that—in other words—nothing will produce the good world but the good man.

These are the principal spiritual handholds I have found to possess enduring value They offer both an exciting challenge and a calm assurance They are the things I believe.

DR. FRED D FAGG, JR's six-foot two-inch frame accords well with his big job as President of the University of Southern California, with its thirty thousand students. In his undergraduate days at the University of Redlands, Dr. Fagg played football He still follows the sport closely, and is a strong defender of athletics as a part of college life. He likes to climb mountains, fish in alpine lakes, and swim in the big, rolling breakers of the Pacific.

Dr. Fagg was a pilot in World War I, and this experience started a life-long interest in aviation An attorney, he helped write laws for the air transportation industry in its infancy. A staunch believer in the American system of free enterprise, Dr Fagg is a director of Freedoms Foundation.

He is a graduate not only of Redlands but of Harvard and Northwestern Universities. He taught economics and law and was Vice-President and Dean of Faculties at Northwestern before coming to U.S.C. in 1947.

I Am Happy with My Time

BY PAT FRANK

In 1945 I followed our armies in their final thrust through Italy, and then flew to Berlin to cover the Potsdam conference. The American correspondents in Berlin were housed in the suburb of Zehlendorf. I was billeted in a typical middle-class home on a shady street. My roommate was Ed Murrow. We were the only two Americans in the house.

The Russians had occupied Zehlendorf before us, and they had stripped this house of linen and blankets, but we had our bedrolls. The elderly couple that owned the house lived over the garage At first these two old people were frightened of us. They had been told the Americans were barbarians. We would wreck their house and take what the Russians had overlooked.

We told the couple to come back and live in their own house. And because Murrow and I had traveled long and far, we carried with us the staples that in those days correspondents did not forget —chocolate, coffee, soap, tea, K-rations, and canned meat and butter. We gave these things to the old people and told them to run the house, and take for themselves whatever they needed. They were pitifully and almost incoherently grateful.

The next night we found flowers in our room, and I knew we had made two friends. In the ruin and bitterness of Berlin, still stinking of death, a vase of flowers was a wondrous thing.

I have seen and talked with the three enemy peoples of World War II—the Germans, the Japanese and the Italians. It has always been my belief that people everywhere are fundamentally alike, and I think that it is proved by the fact that these three enemies are now our allies, actual or potential. It is fundamental that kindness will be repaid with kindness, and hate by hate.

We live in what Toynbee, the great British historian, calls "a time of troubles," but I am happy with my time. Our generation has been bloodied by two wars, and perhaps faces a third, even more frightful. But I would not have lived in another time, for there have been compensations, as small as flowers offered in friendship, and as inspiring as the birth of the United Nations.

If I live in a time of troubles, I also realize that I live in a time of great opportunity. As a reporter and foreign correspondent I was privileged to watch history being made, to see events which have helped to decide whether civilization will stand or fall. I have seen time and again how tremendously important the character of ordinary individuals could be in determining whether our children would live and be proud of us. I know that I cannot escape my responsibility to put the lessons I have learned into action. With all my faults and frailties, I have a duty to myself and to the world I live in. Perhaps I will never know just how important it is, yet I must so live as never to be ashamed of how I fulfilled it.

 PAT FRANK, a native of Chicago, has covered the world as a writer Starting as a reporter in Florida, he later served as chief of the Washington Bureau of the Overseas News Agency, assistant head of O.W.I. operations in the South Pacific, and as war correspondent on the Italian front, in the Middle East and Central Europe.

His wartime impressions and insights have since been fashioned into three novels: *Mr. Adam,* a witty fantasy on the atomic age; *An Affair of State,* a tense story of intrigue in Budapest, and *Hold Back the Night,* a moving tribute to the Americans in the Korean War

Mr. Frank lives with his wife and three sons in Atlantic Beach, Florida. He is now, at forty-five, devoting his entire energies to writing fiction. He works at home, surrounded by books, a typewriter, an ash tray, and a large map of the world.

The Law of the Heart

BY J. GEORGE FREDERICK

AT LONG LAST I have come to a rather simple point as to what I believe. I believe in what I choose to call "The Law of the Heart." In the medical world this phrase, The Law of the Heart, means the great discovery by Professor Ernest Henry Starling of the precise method by which the heart accelerates and retards itself through the heart muscle, also the manner in which it accomplishes the vital two-way exchange of fluids between the bloodstream and the body tissues

In my view of life there is also supremely needful a vital two-way exchange of heart qualities between human beings. Without it the human spirit and relationship to other spirits is lifeless and dangerous. Dependence on head qualities is mechanical and empty, just as we have discovered that babies do not thrive, even with technically expert nursing care, without mother love.

The Law of the Heart, in my belief, then, means that I can achieve greatest physical and mental health, and have the most constructive relations with life and people, if my matured emotional self dominates my motives and actions. When, after due consultation with my head, the true heart speaks, it is the finest and most mellowed judgment that I, human creature, am capable of Man is indivisible, I believe; he is a whole; mind, spirit, body—but with only one real, fully representative voice—the voice of the heart.

There is, in my belief, very suggestive symbolism in the means by which the Law of the Heart operates. We know that man needs to give others weaker, less fortunate, a transfusion of his blood as proof of fellowship. We know that hearts and arteries which are hard and unresponsive can bring the retribution of sudden death. We know that hearts which beat in unison with the problems, pains, miseries and needs of others know celestial music which can never be known to those who do not. We know that hearts capable of

55

quickened pulse at the sight of beauty and nobility, courage and sacrifice, love and tenderness, a child or a sunset, achieve intensities of living—a song in their hearts—unknown to others. We know that those who choke off the heart's native impulses will likely bring on a coronary thrombosis of obstructed emotion which can cripple.

The first Law of the Heart, I feel sure, is to pulsate, to love. To fail to pulsate and love is swift and certain spiritual death. There are far, far too many of us who seem obsessed with self, unable or unwilling to love. The second Law of the Heart, I believe, is to give, and forgive, to sacrifice. The heart is the great supplier and giver to every remote atom in the body. The heart muscle is the strongest in the whole body.

These things I know and believe, and they provide me with the foundation of what I call my humanistic philosophy of life. It works for me. I feel close to the earth with it, yet face uplifted. The heart is closer to everlasting reality, although I am fully aware that I must not let raw emotion masquerade as a heart quality, and that the immature heart can make serious errors. The educated, matured heart is, to my belief, not only the noblest thing in man but also the great hope of the world.

J. GEORGE FREDERICK is president of the Business Bourse, a research and publishing organization A founder of the Better Business Bureaus, he also helped establish the New York Sales-manager's Club. One of his most significant accomplishments was the development of the now highly regarded field of marketing research.

When he finds time from his business, Mr. Frederick likes to cook and has written several cookbooks, including his Long Island Sea Food Cook Book. President of the Gourmet Society of New York, he presides over their famous dinners Always a student of psychology, he is the author of How to Get Tough With Yourself, and What Is Your Emotional Age?

Other members of the busy Frederick family include his wife, Christine, who is a noted household editor, and his daughter, Jean Joyce, an attaché of the United States Embassy in India. His son, the late David Frederick, was general manager of Harper's Magazine.

A Mask Was Stifling Me

BY LUCY FREEMAN

I BELIEVE that everyone wants to love and be loved and that happiness stems from a facing and acceptance of self that allows you to give and receive love

Some think of love as a passionate, hungry, dramatic feeling, all-consuming in intensity and desire. As I see it, this is, rather, immature love; it is a demand on others, not a giving of oneself. Mature love, the love that brings happiness, flows out of an inner fullness, and accepts, understands and is tender toward the other person. It does not ask to be served but only where it may serve.

Six years ago I could hardly breathe because of acute sinus. My stomach was always upset and full of queasiness and I had trouble sleeping, even though I felt exhausted all the time. In desperation, after doctors who treated the physical symptoms failed to ease the pain, I tried psychoanalysis. I was lucky to find a wise, compassionate man who showed me what it meant to be able to trust myself and others.

The physical ills are gone, but more than that, I have at long last started to acquire a philosophy of living. I had never possessed one. I had lived on dogma and dicta which I had accepted unquestioningly through the years, even though I believed little of it, because I feared to question. But by being unable to live naturally and at peace with myself I was flying in the face of nature. She was punishing me with illness and, at the same time, informing me all was not well just in case I wanted to do something about it.

In order to change, I needed help in facing myself. For me it was not easy to "know thyself." All my life I had accepted the lesser of the two evils and run away from self because truth was more dangerous. Once I thought that to survive I had to put on a mask and forget what lay underneath. But masks are false protections and the inner part of me refused to go unheard for ver. It caught up even-

57

tually, and unless it was to master me I had to face such feelings as fear, anger, envy, hatred, jealousy and excessive need for attention. When I realized I could not have done anything else except what I did, I was able to like myself more and be able to like others not for what they could give me but for what I could give to them.

The Bible shows the way to easy, happy living in many of its pages. It advises, "It is more blessed to give than to receive." Those who expect the most are apt to receive the least. I had expected much and was filled with fury because nothing in the outside world relieved my emptiness and despair. Nothing did, either, until I could face the anger and fury, the emptiness and despair, and slowly start to know such new feelings as compassion, conviction, control, calm. I learned, too, of reason—that judicious combination of thought and feeling that enables me to take more responsibility for myself and others, that allows me to slay the ghosts of the past.

For me there is much hard work ahead to achieve greater happiness. Yet, the very struggle I have put into achieving a measure of it makes happiness that much more dear.

◄§ LUCY FREEMAN, who has been a reporter for The New York Times since 1941, was stricken with a variety of physical illnesses, including acute sinus, six years ago Rather than give up her career, she decided to try psychoanalysis as a means of easing the physical pain Last June she published an account of her experiences, Fight Against Fears, believed to be the first report of a specific psychoanalysis written by a patient under her own name

As a child she longed to be a baseball player and this old interest was reflected in one of her recent magazine articles, "Baseball's for Me." Later she wanted to be a marathon dancer but is now content to be a reporter specializing in news of welfare and psychiatry. She says, "I'm more interested in writing about why men murder than the details of the murder. Perhaps, as we arrive at enough convictions about what causes unhappiness, men will stop murdering themselves and others and someday there may be world peace."

Discovery in a Thunderstorm

BY DR. NELSON GLUECK

MANY YEARS AGO I was on a bicycle trip through some exceedingly picturesque countryside. Suddenly, dark clouds piled up overhead and rain began to fall, but strange to relate, several hundred yards ahead of me the sun shone brilliantly. Pedaling, however, as rapidly as I could, I found it impossible to get into the clear. The clouds with their rain kept advancing faster than I could race forward. I continued this unequal contest for an exhausting half hour, before realizing that I could not win my way to the bright area ahead of me.

Then it dawned upon me that I was wasting my strength in unimportant hurry, while paying no attention whatsoever to the landscape for the sake of which I was making the trip. The storm could not last forever and the discomfort was not unendurable. Indeed, there was much to look at which might otherwise have escaped me. As I gazed about with sharpened appreciation, I saw colors and lines and contours that would have appeared differently under brilliant light. The rain mists which now crowned the wooded hills and the fresh clearness of the different greens were entrancing. My annoyance at the rain was gone and my eagerness to escape it vanished. It had provided me with a new view and helped me understand that the sources of beauty and satisfaction may be found close at hand within the range of one's own sensibilities.

It made me think, then and later, about other matters to which this incident was related. It helped me realize that there is no sense in my attempting ever to flee from circumstances and conditions which cannot be avoided but which I might bravely meet and frequently mend and often turn to good account. I know that half the battle is won if I can face trouble with courage, disappointment with spirit, and triumph with humility. It has become ever clearer to me that danger is far from disaster, that defeat may be the forerunner of final victory, and that, in the last analysis, all achievement is perilously fragile unless based on enduring principles of moral conduct.

I have learned that trying to find a carefree world somewhere far off involves me in an endless chase in the course of which the opportunity for happiness and the happiness of attainment are all too often lost in the chase itself. It has become apparent to me that I cannot wipe out the pains of existence by denying them, blaming them largely or completely on others, or running away from them.

The elements of weakness which mark every person cannot absolve me from the burdens and blessings of responsibility for myself and to others. I can magnify but never lessen my problems by ignoring, evading or exorcising them. I believe that my perplexities and difficulties can be considerably resolved, if not completely overcome, by my own attitudes and actions I am convinced that there can be no guarantee of my happiness except that I help evoke and enhance it by the work of my hands and the dictates of my heart and the direction of my striving I believe that deep faith in God is necessary to keep me and hold mankind uncowed and confident under the vagaries and ordeals of mortal experience, and particularly so in this period of revolutionary storm and travail. If my values receive their sanction and strength from relationship to divine law and acceptance of its ethical imperatives, then nothing can really harm me. "The Lord is my shepherd; I shall not want."

NELSON GLUECK, President of Hebrew Union College, was born in Cincinnati, Ohio, in 1900. After graduating from the University of Cincinnati, he went to Germany and took a Ph.D. at the University of Jena Ordained into the rabbinate by the Hebrew Union College in Cincinnati, he became its president in 1947

For many years connected with the American School of Oriental Research in both Jerusalem and Bagdad, Dr Glueck has archaeologically explored more than 1000 ancient sites in the Transjordan. The excavator of King Solomon's port city of Ezion-Geber on the Red Sea, he also discovered King Solomon's copper mines in the Wadi Arabah, and has identified many hitherto lost Biblical cities in the Jordan Valley

The author of many scientific articles and books, including The Other Side of the Jordan and four volumes on Explorations in Eastern Palestine, Dr Glueck has also written The River Jordan, a book that has been characterized as showing "an almost unique combination of learning, personality, and spiritual feeling."

A Sort of Unselfish Selfishness

BY WARD GREENE

WHEN A MAN IS TEN, he has a boy's faith in almost everything, even Santa Claus is a belief he is not quite ready to give up so long as there is a chance the old gentleman may really live and deliver When a man is twenty, he is closer to complete disillusion and stronger conviction than he will probably ever be in his life. This is the age of atheists and agnostics; it is also the age of martyrs. Jesus Christ must have been a very young man when He died on the cross; Joan of Arc, they say, was only nineteen as the flames consumed her. It is in the later years—oh, anywhere from thirty to fifty—that a man at some time stands with the tatters of his hopes and dreams fallen from him and asks himself, "What, indeed, do I believe?"

He is very apt, then, to cling to the words of other men who have written for him the shadowy signposts that come as close as anything to pointing pathways he found best in the past and roads he will trust on the way ahead These words may be mere copybook maxims: that honesty is the best policy, or haste makes waste. They may be a line from Shakespeare—"To thine own self be true"—or from the Bible—"All things whatsoever ye would that men should do to you, do ye even so to them"—or from the poets—"I myself am Heav'n and Hell " They may seem a sort of hodgepodge in a man's mind, yet they can make a pattern not inconsistent and not weak.

So if I believe that I myself am Heaven and Hell, that anything less than honesty to myself and others is a boomerang on them and me; if my translation of the Golden Rule is simple acts of kindness and understanding and compassion, practiced in the hope that they will be shown to me, then I have a way of life that is a sort of unselfish selfishness. The bald statement may sound cynical, but if I can follow that way, I shall not be too unhappy here and I may face death with regret but an untroubled face and a stout heart.

But there are blocks and pitfalls in a way of life, even assuming that a man can adhere to it steadfastly despite his own inclinations to deviate. These obstacles are the work of other men who adhere to other ways. Hence kindness and compassion are not enough.

A man, I believe, must have courage and fortitude and a burning sense of justice, too. There are times we should turn the other cheek, but there are likewise times when we must fight the good fight. When? Well, if a fellow can't find the answer on the signposts or in his heart, I guess he has just got to pray.

WARD GREENE is editor and general manager of one of the world's great newspaper syndicates, King Features. He hails from Georgia and has spent most of his life opposing sham and being curious about people During the twenties he wrote novels, in Greenwich Village. Of the heroine of *Cora Potts*, H. L. Mencken once wrote: "That gal is one of my favorites in American fiction."

Of this man who has written seven novels, two plays, a children's book and a Disney movie, the great Damon Runyon once remarked that Greene would seem to be "quite at home passing the collection box in a Baptist congregation."

Mr. Greene is a medium-sized, bespectacled man with a blunt but engaging manner. He plays the harmonica with skill, and tells jokes lustily. All his life he has never wanted to be anything but a newspaperman He says he would like to have as his epitaph: "Ward Greene: a good reporter."

The Art of Bouncing Back

BY JOYCE GRENFELL

I THINK the center of my faith is an absolute certainty of good. Like everyone else, I get low and there are times when I feel as if I have my fins on backwards and am swimming upstream in heavy boots. But even in these dark times, even though I feel cut off, perhaps, and alone, I am aware—even if distantly—that I am part of a whole and that the whole is true and real and good.

I have never had any difficulty in believing in God. I don't believe in a personal God and I don't quite see how it is possible to believe in a God who knows both good and evil and yet to trust in Him. I believe in God, good, in One Mind, and I believe we are all subject to and part of this oneness.

It's taken me time to understand words like "tolerance" and "understanding." I have given lip service to "tolerance" and to "understanding" for years but only now do I think I begin to understand a little what they mean. If we are all one of another, and this, though uncomfortably, is probably the case, then sooner or later we have got to come to terms with each other. I believe in the individuality of man, and it is only by individual experience that we can, any of us, make a contribution to understanding.

I've always been a bit confused about self and egotism because I instinctively felt both were barriers to understanding. And so in a sense they are.

I used to worry a lot about personality and that sort of egotism. I noticed that certain artists—musicians, for instance—would allow their personalities to get between the music and the listener. But others, greater and therefore humbler, became clear channels through which the music was heard unimpeded. And it occurred to me, not very originally, that the good we know in man is from God so it is a good thing to try to keep oneself as clear as possible from the

63

wrong sort of self. And it's not very easy, particularly if you are on the stage!

I am one of those naturally happy people who even when they get low soon bounce back. In minor things like housekeeping and keeping in sight of letters to be answered I am a Planny-Annie That is to say I get through the chores in order to enjoy the space beyond. But I do find that, believing in the operation of good as I do, I cannot make plans—important ones, I mean—but I must prepare the ground and then leave the way free as far as possible. This, of course, means being fearless and isn't fatalistic, because you see I believe that when I am faithful enough to be still and to allow things to happen serenely, they do. And this being still isn't a negative state but an awareness of one's true position.

Friends are the most important things in my life—that and the wonder of being necessary to someone. But these things pass and in the end one is alone with God. I'm not nearly ready for that yet, but I do see it with my heart's eye.

I don't understand it entirely, but I believe there is only now and our job is to recognize and rejoice in this now. Now . . . not, of course, the man-measured now of Monday, Friday or whenever, but the now of certain truth. That doesn't change. Surely everything has been done—is done. Our little problem is to reveal and enjoy.

◄§ JOYCE GRENFELL had studied dramatics and singing but with no thought of professionally exploiting her talents. One evening, at a party, she entertained her fellow guests, among whom was Herbert Farjeon. He persuaded her to take a part in his forthcoming *Little Revue* Her success in this production established her in the English entertainment world.

Miss Grenfell has since appeared in a number of other intimate revues, including Noel Coward's *Sigh No More*.

She has also appeared in films and on television, American audiences having seen her as Miss Gossage in the picture *The Happiest Days of Your Life*

She combines an analytical eye for character with a way of bringing it to life that is unique. Whether the person she creates is a gawky schoolgirl, a factory woman, or a retired child's nurse, the portrait is devastatingly true, and leaves her audiences feeling that "only Joyce Grenfell could have done it just like that."

A Morning Prayer in a Little Church

BY HELEN HAYES

ONCE, years ago, I got into a dogfight. I was wheeling a baby carriage, my pet cocker spaniel trotting beside me. Without warning, three dogs—an Afghan, a St. Bernard and a Dalmatian—pounced on the cocker and started tearing him to pieces. I shrieked for help. Two men in a car stopped, looked, and drove on.

When I saw that I was so infuriated that I waded in and stopped the fight myself. My theatrical training never stood me in better stead. My shouts were so authoritative, my gestures so arresting, I commanded the situation like a lion-tamer and the dogs finally slunk away.

Looking back, I think I acted less in anger than from a realization that I was on my own, that if anybody was going to help me at that moment, it had to be myself.

Life seems to be a series of crises that have to be faced. In summoning strength to face them, though, I once fooled myself into an exaggerated regard of my own importance. I felt very independent. I was only distantly aware of other people. I worked hard and was "successful." In the theater, I was brought up in the tradition of service. The audience pays its money and you are expected to give your best performance—both on and off the stage. So I served on committees, and made speeches, and backed causes. But somehow the meaning of things escaped me.

When my daughter died of polio, everybody stretched out a hand to help me, but at first I couldn't seem to bear the touch of anything, even the love of friends; no support seemed strong enough.

While Mary was still sick, I used to go early in the morning to a little church near the hospital to pray. There the working people came quietly to worship. I had been careless with my religion, I had rather cut God out of my life, and I didn't have the nerve at the time to ask Him to make my daughter well—I only asked Him to help me understand, to let me come in and reach Him. I prayed there every morning and I kept looking for a revelation, but nothing happened.

And then, much later, I discovered that it *had* happened, right there in the church I could recall, vividly, one by one, the people I had seen there—the solemn laborers with tired looks, the old women with gnarled hands. Life had knocked them around, but for a brief moment they were being refreshed by an ennobling experience. It seemed as they prayed their worn faces lighted up and they became the very vessels of God. Here was my revelation. Suddenly I realized I was one of them. In my need I gained strength from the knowledge that they too had needs, and I felt an interdependence with them. I experienced a flood of compassion for people. I was learning the meaning of "Love thy neighbor. . . ."

Truths as old and simple as this began to light up for me like the faces of the men and women in the little church. When I read the Bible now, as I do frequently, I take the teachings of men like Jesus and David and St. Paul as the helpful advice of trusted friends about how to live. They understand that life is full of complications and often heavy blows and they are showing me the wisest way through it. I must help myself, yes, but I am not such a self-contained unit that I can live aloof, unto myself. This was the meaning that had been missing before. the realization that I was a living part of God's world of people.

◄§ HELEN HAYES, a first lady of the American theater, began to act almost as soon as she could walk. While doing an impersonation at a ball when she was still a child, she was observed by Producer Lew Fields, who later gave her a part in one of his musicals.

Sometime afterwards she appeared in Sir James M. Barrie's *Dear Brutus* and was immediately acclaimed "the greatest young actress in New York City." During a rehearsal of *We Moderns* in 1924, she met the playwright Charles MacArthur, whom she later married

Particularly remembered for her illustrious performance in *Victoria Regina*, she has more recently appeared on the New York stage in *Mrs Mc-Thing*. She has also made many memorable films More than one young actress today has a helping hand from Helen Hayes to thank for her success. Miss Hayes is just over five feet tall, attractive, and vivacious She lives with her family in Nyack, New York

We Can't Just Play with Spools

BY GENERAL LEWIS B. HERSHEY

I BELIEVE that the greatest frontier of our ignorance lies in the relationship of man to man. I do not discount the marvelous development in the world of things, nor do I devaluate the contributions of those who made these developments possible. Yet all these are but means, and unless we can learn to shape and to control them to ends that are constructive for the inhabitants of this earth, material miracles become not only futile but worse; worse, because they provide more means of destruction. I believe the frontier of human relationship can be extended. It will not be easy to do so. Man must learn more about himself than he already knows. The human emotions and the meaning of human behavior present difficulties in measurement much greater than those encountered in learning to measure steel or gold.

Perhaps the greatest impediment to the advancement of knowledge about us has been the fact that we have assumed we know. The man who can predict accurately the smell or color of the vapor which arises when two substances are mixed excites his fellow citizens far more than one who tries to predict the result of the clash of two personalities. In the second phenomenon we tend to solve by one of two methods. We dismiss it as unpredictable prior to the clash, or, afterwards, we declare the result to have been inevitable and expected by everyone. In either case we are denying our ignorance.

We shall have overcome one of the largest obstacles to a solution of man's favorable relationship with man when we know and acknowledge how little we know about ourselves. The step to follow our admission of ignorance is to seek the knowledge and understanding that we have concluded we do not have. This will be a long and difficult road, as long perhaps as from learning how to make fire to learning how to fission the atom. Man must turn his eyes and interest inward. He has already made more gadgets than he understands or knows how to control. He resembles a child after Christmas, unable to manage the strange and complicated machine toys that had challenged the interest of his parents. Our acceptance that we do not know and must seek to learn cannot wait. We have not the choice of the child. We cannot play with spools and leave the more complicated machines to our parents.

Lewis B Hershey, Major General, United States Army, has been Director of Selective Service since July, 1941. By the time the war ended he and his staff had directly provided more than ten million men for the Armed Forces.

A big man, neither stocky nor slim and of ruddy complexion, his naturalness of manner puts everyone about him completely at ease. His attack on every problem is characterized by keen insight into the human elements involved.

General Hershey applies a homely philosophy to everything he says and everything he does. This philosophy finds expression in a rich humor, often sly, but always good-natured, revealing his love of people, his kindliness and his tolerance. The General has written extensively on subjects relating to Selective Service. He lives in Bethesda, Maryland

Do You Know Your Special Talent?

BY ANNE HEYWOOD

WHAT I AM ABOUT to say may appear to be plugging my own business, but it's what I know best . . and I believe it deeply and sincerely.

I believe that every human being has a talent—something that he can do better than anyone else. And I believe that the distinction between so-called "creative" talents and ordinary run-of-the-mill talents is an unnecessary and man-made distinction. I have known exterminators, typists, waitresses and machinists whose creative joy and self-fulfillment in their work could not be surpassed by Shakespeare's or Einstein's.

When I was in my teens, I read a quotation from Thomas Carlyle: "Blessed is he who has found his work. Let him ask no other blessedness." At the time I thought that was a pretty grim and dreary remark, but I know now that Mr. Carlyle was right. When you find the thing that you can do better than anything else in the world, then all the wonderful by-products fall in line—financial security, happy personal relationships, peace of mind. I believe that until you find it your search for the by-products will be in vain.

I also believe that in the process of searching, no experience is ever wasted, unless we allow ourselves to run out of hope. In my own case I had thirty-four different jobs before I found the right one. Many of these jobs were heart-breakingly difficult. A few of them involved working with unscrupulous and horribly unpleasant people. Yet, in looking back, I can see that the most unpleasant of these jobs, in many cases, gave me the biggest dividends—the most valuable preparation for my proper life work.

And I have seen this happen in the destinies of hundreds of people. Periods which they thought were hopeless, dark and of no possible practical value have turned out to be the most priceless experiences they ever had. One of my friends is a famous package designer for American industry. She was just given a promotion for which she competed with six well-qualified designers. Her past, like all of ours, had its good times and its bad times. One of the worst of the bad times was a period when she lost her husband and was left with two small children to support. She took a clerking job in a grocery store because her apartment was on the floor above it and between customers she could run up and keep an eye on the babies It was a two-year period of great despair, during which she was constantly on the verge of suicide Yet the other day when she told me of her promotion to the top package design post, she exclaimed in astonishment, "And do you know that the single factor which swung it in my favor was that I alone had over-the-counter experience with the customers who buy our packaged foods!"

When people talk about the sweet uses of adversity, I think they unduly stress a grim and hopeless resignation, a conviction that, like unpleasant medicine, it is somehow "good for us." But I think it is much more than that. I know that the unhappy periods of our lives offer us concrete and useful plus values, chief among them a heightened understanding and compassion for others. We may not see it at the time, we may consider the experience entirely wasted, but, as Emerson says, "The years teach much which the days never know."

⚜ ANNE HEYWOOD, Founder and Director of the Career-Changing Clinic in New York City, is a young woman in her middle thirties, born in Keokuk, Iowa, and mother of an eight-year-old son With a management engineer father and a naval officer husband, she traveled throughout the United States and held thirty-four different jobs in widely diversified fields.

All this experience added up when she joined the staff of a busy employment agency right after World War II There she saw hundreds of returning servicemen and women who were, as she says, "bound and determined not to go back into Daddy's plumbing supply business." And so she opened the Career-Changing Clinic, which has helped thousands of businessmen and women—and housewives as well—to find new fields. She is the author of a book, *There Is a Right Job for Every Woman*

Escape the Dark Destructive Force

BY ROBERT HILLYER

"I FEEL the coming glory of the light" This last line of Edwin Arlington Robinson's sonnet "Credo" expresses the general basis of my belief. It is my task to clear away the debris of dead emotions, regrets and petty ambitions that the quickening light may come through. The five senses and the mystery of the breath draw in the wonder of the world, and, with that, the glory of God. I may seldom rise to moments of exaltation, but I try to keep myself prepared for them. Thus I oppose the desire for oblivion that gnaws at our roots even as the light is summoning us to bloom.

The desire for oblivion conspires against the soul from outer circumstances and also from within oneself. Its agents are worry and resentment, envy and show. Its impulse is to seek things that are equally disappointing whether they are missed or acquired. Its result is an abject conviction that everything is futile. By meditation and prayer I can escape that dark, destructive force and win my way back to the beauties of the world and the joy of God.

I believe in my survival after death. Like many others before me, I have experienced "intimations of immortality." I can no more explain these than the brown seed can explain the flowering tree. Deep in the soil in time's midwinter, my very stirring and unease seem a kind of growing pain toward June.

As to orthodox belief, I am an Episcopalian, like my family before me. I can repeat the Creed without asking too much margin for personal interpretation. To me it is a pattern, like the sonnet form in poetry, for the compact expression of faith. There are other patterns for other people, and I have no quarrel with these. "By many paths we reach the single goal."

I believe in the good intentions of others, and I trust people instinctively. My trust has often been betrayed in petty ways, and, once or twice, gravely. I cannot stop trusting people because suspicion is contrary to my nature. Nor would I, because the number of people who have justified my trust are ten to one to those who have abused it. And I know that on occasion I have myself, perhaps inadvertently, failed to live up to some trust reposed in me.

That the universe has a purposeful movement toward spiritual perfection seems to me logical, unless we are all cells in the brain of an idiot. A belief in spiritual as well as physical evolution has sustained me in an optimism still unshaken by cynics. There may be setbacks of a century or even centuries, but they seem small reverses when measured against the vast prospect of human progress or even the record of it to this point.

I am blest with a buoyant temperament and enjoy the pleasures of this earth For daily living I would say. One world at a time. I do not wish my life to be cluttered with material things; on the other hand, I do not wish to anticipate, by fanatical self-denial, the raptures to come. Sufficient unto the day is the good thereof.

◆§ ROBERT HILLYER, Pulitzer Prize winner in poetry, was born in East Orange, New Jersey, in 1895. Following his graduation from Harvard in 1917, he was commissioned in the A.E F. and served two years. On his return to this country he taught at Harvard Later the University honored him by making him Boyleston Professor of Rhetoric and Oratory, a chair he continues to occupy.

His first book, *Sonnets and Other Lyrics*, was published when he was twenty-two Various volumes of verse followed, along with a novel, *Riverhead*, in 1932 His *Collected Verse* in 1933 won him the Pulitzer Prize the following year.

Mr. Hillyer is now President of the Poetry Society of America His work is considered to be in the sound tradition of English verse His most recent book is a volume of lyrics, *The Suburb by the Sea* He is married, has one son, and lives with his family in Greenwich, Connecticut.

You Cannot "Fix" a Real Faith

BY NAT HOLMAN

WHEN I LEARNED that members of my team, boys whom I had trusted and to whom I had devoted intense training and guidance—when I learned that these boys had been "fixed" by professional gamblers, my faith and belief in the basic integrity of youth received a severe blow. Any weaker confidence in the principles upon which I have tried to base my life might well have folded under its force. Yet I can honestly say that my belief in the real decency of the great majority of our young men and the value of athletics is as strong as ever. The indiscretions of a few youngsters cannot destroy a faith built up by thirty-four years of experience with other boys who have justified that faith.

Throughout the years I've seen thousands of boys getting important training on the athletic field. I have seen them learn honesty and fair play, and I've seen them learn to subordinate themselves for the benefit of their team. What is more important, I've seen them take the lessons they have learned here into the situations they've had to face in later life. Many of the boys I've helped to teach have become outstanding members of their communities.

I realize that the responsibilities of any teacher are great and that those of a coach who spends more time with his pupils than any other teacher are even greater. Not only do I spend more time, but I feel emotionally closer to them, seeing and sustaining my students when they lose as well as when they win.

Because of this peculiarly intimate relationship with the members of my team in their most impressionable and formative years, I know that I can exercise great influence for good or bad on them. I try by the example of my own character and actions to set them a standard of moral behavior. For this reason, I have always tried to be very clear in my own mind about the principles in which I believe.

Take the desire to win, fundamental with every competitor. Nat-

73

urally, it's important to me, both as a player and coach and as a human being. I believe the competitive urge is a fine, wholesome direction of energy But I also realize that the desire to win must be wedded to an ideal, an ethical way of life It must never become so strong that it dwarfs every other aspect of the game or of life.

As a coach I have always tried to emphasize that winning is not enough. The game must be played right. I have often said that I would rather see my teams lose a game in which they played well than win with a sloppy performance that reflected no credit, except that it was sufficient to win. So I've tried to develop a way of thinking that sees life, and the things I do, as a whole, with every act relating to another set. This puts things in true perspective.

I believe in the resilience, in the bounce, of youth. I get rich satisfaction from working with young people, providing leadership and friendship during the tortuous but exciting years that shape them toward maturity. I honestly think no more worthwhile activity could occupy my time. Edwin Markham has summed it up better than I could. He wrote:

> "There is a destiny that makes us brothers,
>   None goes his way alone.
> All that we send into the lives of others,
>   Comes back into our own."

◄§ NAT HOLMAN, legendary star of the original Celtics and dean of American basketball coaches, learned the game on the playgrounds of New York's lower East Side Today he is one of basketball's immortals He has just concluded his thirty-fourth year as head coach of basketball and professor of hygiene at the College of the City of New York.

As author, lecturer, and coach, his contributions to the game have been world-wide. The Mexican and Israeli governments invited him to their respective countries to teach the more advanced techniques of the sport. His four textbooks on basketball, including *Scientific Basketball* and *Holman on Basketball*, have been translated into several foreign languages.

Past president of the National Collegiate Basketball Coaches Association, his greatest triumph was in 1950 when his team won the unprecedented double championship of both the NCAA and National Invitational Tournament.

I See No Doom Down an Alley

BY HERBERT HOOVER

MY PROFESSIONAL TRAINING was in science and engineering. That is a training in the search for truth and its application to the use of mankind. With the growth of science we have had a continuous contention from a tribe of atheistic and agnostic philosophers that there is an implacable conflict between science and religion in which religion will be vanquished. I do not believe it.

I believe not only that religious faith will be victorious, but that it is vital to mankind that it shall be. We may differ in form and particulars in our religious faith Those are matters which are sacred to each of our inner sanctuaries. It is our privilege to decline to argue them Their real demonstration is the lives that we live.

But there is one foundation common to all religious faith.

Our discoveries in science have proved that all the way from the galaxies in the heavens to the constitution of the atom, the universe is controlled by inflexible laws. Somewhere a Supreme Power created these laws. At some period, man was differentiated from the beasts and was endowed with a spirit from which sprung conscience, idealism and spiritual yearnings. It is impossible to believe that there is not here a divine touch and a purpose from the Creator of the Universe. I believe we can express these things only in religious faith.

From their religious faith, the Founding Fathers enunciated the most fundamental law of human progress since the Sermon on the Mount, when they stated that man received from the Creator certain inalienable rights and that these rights should be protected from the encroachment of others by law and justice.

The agnostic and atheistic philosophers have sought to declaim progress in terms of materialism alone. But from whence come the morals, the spiritual yearnings, the faith, the aspirations to justice and freedom of mind which have been the roots of our progress?

Always growing societies record their faith in God; decaying societies lack faith and deny God. But America is not a decaying society. It remains strong. Its faith is in compassion and in God's intelligent mercy.

◄§ HERBERT HOOVER was born a poor boy, in West Branch, Iowa, and brought up a Quaker. Working his way through Stanford University, he was graduated in mining engineering (the first of some fifty-eight degrees he now holds) Later he went to Australia to introduce American engineering methods on behalf of a British firm. He came back and married Lou Henry, his college sweetheart. He and Mrs Hoover raised their children while traveling the world over. Few men have known a happier married life

When the First World War broke out, his Quaker "concern" caused him to give up a business in which he had amassed a fortune, and take on the great job of Belgian War Relief Later he became Secretary of Commerce and, in 1929, President of the United States. It is perhaps not generally known, but Mr Hoover drew no salary as President, turning the money over to charity. Since the death of Mrs Hoover in 1944, this revered elder statesman has lived in the Waldorf-Astoria Towers, in New York, working on his autobiography

The Hole in the Enemy's Armor

BY LEWIS M. HOSKINS

DURING THE helter-skelter days of guerrilla civil fighting in China, our Quaker unit found it hard to carry on the desperately needed medical work unobstructed. Appreciated by both sides, it still fell victim to the uncertainties of the tide of battle. For example, a Quaker hospital changed hands six times in ten days but carried on its medical work throughout! The necessity of identification by both armies made necessary occasional trips across no man's land. In such cases, if it was somewhat ticklish leaving one side, it was more difficult to make contact with the army of the other side. I remember one such trip to negotiate with Communist authorities regarding the medical needs of this fought-over area. We were well into disputed territory when a Chinese member of the unit and I were captured by a lone Communist sentry He was only a youngster of perhaps fourteen and was dangerous primarily because he was badly frightened. I was acutely conscious of the barriers which divided us. In addition to the normal ones of nationality, race and language were the unnatural ones of fear, suspicion and hatred produced by propaganda. I was a representative of the nation he had been told was the enemy of his people. Though unarmed, I was suspected of trickery and deceit.

After considerable palaver, the young Communist soldier agreed to permit my Chinese colleague to return for the other members of our negotiating party while I would be held hostage For over twenty minutes as I faced this intense Chinese lad, covering me with his rifle, I tried to win his confidence through the persuasion of open-heartedness. I hoped to penetrate to his better nature through the power of friendship. As I talked haltingly with him in Chinese about everyday things, reassuring him of my good will and desire to help his people, I fell upon a device to reach through the artificial barriers and touch his human and normal side. I showed him a picture of my

77

young daughter and then asked him about his own family. He told of a baby sister at home and an older brother also in the army. Unconsciously, it seemed, he put down his gun. In my halting Chinese I told him about the work of the Quaker unit, why we were there, and how we hoped to bring friendship and good will with our technical assistance.

No matter how encrusted had become his suspicion and hatred, long built up by propaganda, it was possible to reach through to his common humanity and to elicit a friendly response from his deeper spirit. When the rest of the Quaker party had arrived, the young soldier agreed to pilot us back to his headquarters, where we could carry out our vital negotiations.

I cite this personal incident to illustrate my faith in the possibility, under God, of that vital deeper communication among all members of our common humanity, which is necessary for peace and understanding.

LEWIS M. HOSKINS is executive secretary of the American Friends Service Committee, in Philadelphia, a group whose contribution to world peace won it a Nobel Prize. Born in a small Oregon town, he has acquired a world outlook through his extensive travels and his years of foreign service.

He was graduated from Pacific University, went on to do graduate work at Haverford and the University of Michigan. He holds a Master's and a Doctor's degree in history, and was for a time professor of history and dean of faculty at Pacific College. His teaching career also embraced a period in China, where he taught American history and sociology in Shanghai.

From 1945 to 1948 he served with a Quaker unit in China, his first job being manager of a hospital in Honan Province. He has organized and directed many relief projects in Europe and the Far East. Mr. Hoskins is the father of three daughters. His home is in Wallingford, Pennsylvania.

Taxi Drivers Are People Too

BY JOHN HUGHES

I BELIEVE honesty is one of the greatest gifts there is.

I know they call it a lot of fancy names these days like integrity and forthrightness. But it doesn't make any difference what they call it, it's still what makes a man a good citizen.

This is my code and I try to live by it.

I've been in the taxicab business for thirty-five years and I know there is a lot about it that is not so good. Taxicab drivers have to be rough-and-tumble fellows to be able to take it in New York. You got to be tough to fight the New York traffic eight hours a day, these days. Because taxi drivers are tough, people get the wrong impression that they are bad. Taxi drivers are just like other people. Most of them will shake down as honest fellows. You read in the papers almost every week where a taxi driver turns in money or jewels or bonds, stuff like that, that people leave in their cabs. If they weren't honest, you wouldn't be reading those stories in the newspapers.

One time in Brooklyn I found an emerald ring in my cab. I remembered helping a lady with a lot of bundles that day, so I went back to where I had dropped her off. It took me almost two days to trace her down in order to return her ring to her. I didn't get as much as thank you Still, I felt good because I had done what was right. I think I felt better than she did.

I was born and raised in Ireland and lived there until I was nineteen years old. I came to this country in 1913 where I held several jobs to earn a few dollars before enlisting in World War Number I. After being discharged I bought my own cab and have owned one ever since. It hasn't been too easy at times but my wife takes care of our money and we have a good bit put away for a rainy day.

When I first started driving a cab, Park Avenue was mostly a bunch of coal yards. Hoofer's Brewery was right next to where the Waldorf-Astoria is now. I did pretty well, even in those days.

In all my years of driving a taxicab, I have never had any trouble with the public, not even with drunks. Even if they get a little headstrong once in a while, I just agree with them and then they behave themselves.

People ask me about tips As far as I know, practically everyone will give you something. Come to think of it, most Americans are pretty generous. I always try to be nice to everyone, whether they tip or not.

I believe in God and try to be a good member of my parish. I try to act toward others like I think God wants me to act. I have been trying this for a long time, and the longer I try the easier it gets.

~§ JOHN HUGHES has driven a taxicab about the streets of New York for thirty-five years, during which he has had time to think a lot of thoughts. Born on a picturesque farm in County Monaghan, Ireland, he was orphaned at two He came to this country as a young lad and he enlisted in the Army, serving during the First World War. He was honorably discharged in 1918.

He is of slight build but youthful participation in active sports helped him develop a strong constitution. He has a will and determination to match, and they work together to support his many firmly held beliefs. Having a great faith in young people, he insists that there is no such thing as an innately bad boy, that a boy needs only the opportunity to develop his abilities in the right environment. Mr. Hughes describes himself as "just about what you would call an average American citizen."

Learning to Get Out of the Way

BY ALDOUS HUXLEY

IN EVERY ONE of the higher religions there is a strain of infinite optimism on the one hand and, on the other, of a profound pessimism. In the depths of our being, they all teach, there is an inner Light—but an inner Light which our egotism keeps, for most of the time, in a state of more or less complete eclipse If, however, it so desires, the ego can get out of the way, so to speak, can dis-eclipse the Light and become identified with its divine source. Hence the unlimited optimism of the traditional religions. Their pessimism springs from the observed fact that, though all are called, few are chosen—for the sufficient reason that few choose to be chosen.

To me, this older conception of man's nature and destiny seems more realistic, more nearly in accord with the given facts, than any form of modern utopianism.

In the Lord's Prayer we are taught to ask for the blessing which consists in not being led into temptation. The reason is only too obvious. When temptations are very great or unduly prolonged, most persons succumb to them To devise a perfect social order is probably beyond our powers, but I believe that it is perfectly possible for us to reduce the number of dangerous temptations to a level far below that which is tolerated at the present time.

A society so arranged that there shall be a minimum of dangerous temptations—this is the end towards which, as a citizen, I have to strive. In my efforts to that end, I can make use of a great variety of means. Do good ends justify the use of intrinsically bad means? On the level of theory, the point can be argued indefinitely. In practice, meanwhile, I find that the means employed invariably determine the nature of the end achieved. Indeed, as Mahatma Gandhi was never tired of insisting, the means are the end in its preliminary stages. Men have put forth enormous efforts to make their world a better place to live in; but except in regard to gadgets, plumbing and

81

hygiene, their success has been pathetically small. "Hell," as the proverb has it, "is paved with good intentions." And so long as we go on trying to realize our ideals by bad or merely inappropriate means, our good intentions will come to the same bad ends. In this consists the tragedy and the irony of history.

Can I, as an individual, do anything to make future history a little less tragic and less ironic than history past and present? I believe I can. As a citizen, I can use all my intelligence and all my good will to develop political means that shall be of the same kind and quality as the ideal ends which I am trying to achieve. And as a person, as a psycho-physical organism, I can learn how to get out of the way, so that the divine source of my life and consciousness can come out of eclipse and shine through me

§ ALDOUS HUXLEY, grandson of the great scientist, was born in Surrey, England, but now lives in Los Angeles He describes himself as fifty-eight years old, 6 feet 4 inches tall, and narrow in proportion—in brief, an extreme ectomorph with all the traits that go with this physique.

A prolific writer, he is the author of a brilliant group of novels including Crome Yellow, Point Counterpoint, and Brave New World He refers to himself as an essayist who writes novels, and as an amateur philosopher whose books represent a series of attempts to discover artistic methods for expressing the general idea in the particular instance.

In Madrid's Prado, says Mr Huxley, there is a drawing by Goya of an ancient man hobbling along on two sticks. Under it is the legend· Aun aprendo—"I'm still learning." If ours were still the age of heraldry, these words and the accompanying image would be his crest and motto, he says.

The Soundest Investment of All

BY C. JARED INGERSOLL

I FEEL very presumptuous and uncomfortable about trying to explain out loud the things I believe in. But I do think that all human problems are in some way related to each other, so perhaps if people compare their experiences they may discover something in common in hunting the answers.

I am a very fortunate man for I lead a full and what is for me a happy life. I say this even though I happen to have had, in the course of it, a couple of severe personal blows My first wife collapsed and died one day while she and I were ice-skating, after eighteen years of a most happy existence together. My only son, a sergeant in the Army combat engineers, was killed in Italy in the last war Nonetheless, these tragedies did not throw me completely and I have been able to fill my life anew with happiness.

I do not mean to sound calloused. Those blows hurt me deeply. I guess that two basically important things helped me most to recover. One is the fact that I have come to see life as a gamble. The other is a belief in what some people call the hereafter. I try to live fully so that when my luck changes there will be little room for regret or recrimination over time lost or misspent. My belief in the hereafter is wrapped in the intangible but stubborn thoughts of a layman. Very likely I would get lost in trying to describe or defend, by cold logic, my belief in God but nobody could argue me out of it.

I have come to believe that I owe life as much as it owes me, and I suppose that explains the fine satisfaction I get out of endeavoring to do a job to the best of what ability I have, and out of helping somebody else

As a kid I used to ride a rake in the hayfields. I got a tremendous kick out of trying to sweep every field clean as a whistle. Here I made a surprising and happy discovery: that there could be actual enjoyment in the exercise of thoroughness and responsibility, that duty didn't have to be a drudge

I don't know exactly why, but I like to do things for other people. Not only family responsibilities, work on a hospital board and various church organizations but also the most inconsequential things that might hardly seem worth the time. My office happens to be on Independence Square and now and then I have occasion to direct a tourist to the Liberty Bell or fill him in on a little of the history of Philadelphia. The tourist doesn't seem to mind and it makes me feel good. I'm afraid I'm not very profound. I have tried to comprehend why something so simple and so sound as the Golden Rule is so often forgotten or held in disrepute I can only say—and I say this quite selfishly—that I have found it a good investment. It has paid me a very high return, undoubtedly more than I deserve.

C. JARED INGERSOLL, a graduate of Princeton, is a successful railroad executive. He heads a system of railroads in the Southwest, serves on the Board of the Pennsylvania Railroad. (He is six feet six inches tall and finds that berths on trains are almost always too short and seats in planes equally cramped for accommodating his outsize frame) A director also of the United States Steel Corporation, the Atlantic Refining Company, the Insurance Company of North America, and the Phelps Dodge Corporation, he is intensely interested in church work and in hospital activities in the Philadelphia area.

During World War I Mr Ingersoll served in the Navy In the last war he headed the Army's Philadelphia Ordnance District, which procured over three billion dollars' worth of war matériel

His private interests center in agriculture and fishing He claims there is no surer panacea for worry than to wade waist-high into a cold trout stream in the early spring.

Fixing Up the Run-Down Places

BY DR. DAVID DALLAS JONES

EVERY LIFE coheres around certain fundamental core ideas whether we realize it or not. If I were asked to state the ideas around which my life and my life's work have been built it would seem that they were very simple ideas. An old professor of mine used to say that "effort counts." "The surest thing in the world," he would say, "next to death is that effort counts." This I believe with all my heart. We seldom realize the sense of glow, the sense of growing self-esteem, the sense of achievement, which can come from doing a job well Just working at a thing with enthusiasm and with a belief that the job may be accomplished, however uncertain the outcome, lends zest to life.

If I were to start life again, I think I would do just what I have done in the past—this past having been done by mere chance. I would start at some task which very much needed to be done I would start in a place which was run down and I would believe with all my heart that if the thing needed to be done and if effort were put into it, results would come for human good.

Too, from the outset, my wife and I have had the feeling that no matter what else we did in life, we had to devote our best thinking and our best living to our children. Now that they are all grown, we have sincere satisfaction in the fact that trying to do a job and trying to earn a living did not take away from us this urgency to be and do so that our children could have a feeling of the importance of integrity, honesty and straightforwardness in life. It seems to me far too often this is overlooked We people in public life do the jobs we have to do and fail to save our own children. This second thing is important—doing the task you have to do but beginning at home to bring peace, love, happiness and contentment to those whom God has given you.

The third idea, around which I have tried to live and work, is that there is an overshadowing Providence that cares for one. Ofttimes

85

our struggles are too intense, too "eager beaverish" when, as a matter of fact, time and God can solve many problems Never in my life have I gotten away from the idea that God cares and that He provides that the forces of good in the world are greater than the forces of evil and that if we will lend ourselves to those forces, in the long run we have greater joy and happiness in the thing which we try to achieve This I learned from my mother as a boy. Although she was ill and although we were poor—as poor as people can be—I do not now recall a moment of discouragement in her presence. There was always an overpowering belief that God was in His heaven and that, as Joe Louis said, "God is on our side "

These things I believe with all my heart.

§ DR. DAVID D. JONES, who holds degrees from Wesleyan, Columbia and Howard, is President of Bennett College in Greensboro, North Carolina.

When he came to Bennett in 1926 he had served as Executive Secretary of the YMCA in St. Louis, and with the Commission on Interracial Relations in Atlanta, but had virtually no experience in the field of education He brought with him, however, ideas which have borne fruit through the years.

The idea on which Dr. Jones' philosophy is based is that of the dignity and worth of the individual. This emphasis on the individual is particularly important at Bennett College. Dr. Jones puts it this way "People have a sense of their own dignity and worth only insofar as they have opportunities to make a contribution of their own." Putting his philosophy into effect has has resulted in a close relationship within the "Bennett family"—students, faculty and administration.

Revelations on a Bomb Run

BY CAPTAIN LLOYD JORDAN

ONE DAY while piloting a bomber through the war skies of Europe I came to believe in the immortality of man. There was not any melodrama attached to this awakening. Only through the thousand details of a mind absorbed in a bomb run came the discovery of a single fact: "Ye shall know the truth, and the truth shall make you free."

Below me were the Alps, and the vision of Hannibal crossing them in his time of war flashed through my mind, followed in rapid succession by the remembrance of all the histories of wars. I looked at the bomber machinery about me and at the battle signs of destruction below and realized this was only one of the thousands of wars man has been engaged in, and *still* he has flourished. So then, like the warm sun and friendly heaven and God's other features about me, man, too, must be permanent. The warmth that came into the subzero cockpit with this divine realization made me know that here, at least for me, was the key to a happiness which had been missing before The feeling of a day-to-day existence without hope for the tomorrow changed to a sense of security in the knowledge of having a future. With this truth in mind, one cannot help but try to make a better world to live in.

This awakening came late to me, but with my children it will not be left to happenstance for I have long since begun to show them the tying in of man's immortality with the ageless evidences which are everywhere about us—the Great Artist's glorious paintings of the heavens at sunrise and sunset. The delicate fragrance of a rose. The simple miracle of a newly born lamb. The massive majesty of snow-capped purple mountains. The mysterious many-faced sea hiding a thousand other worlds beneath its cloak. The twinkling lights from stars a billion miles away.

They have learned these things are of God and are immortal just as the music and the paintings of the old masters are God-given and ageless.

"But, Daddy," they have asked me, "the papers say the atom bomb will kill off the human race someday. Is that so?"

How certainly I can assure them now, believing in the imperishability of man as I do, "People said that when the spear came into existence. And the bow and arrow And guns and bullets. And planes and bombs. But there has been someone more powerful than all these forces and so we are here today greater in number, healthier in body and more advanced in science and learning than ever. Have patience with all this hysteria," I tell them. "After all, mankind is only a youngster like one of you. The earth is an unknown millions of years old while man is a mere six thousand years of age. Mankind is still growing up, comparatively, and his growth can be likened to your own It's like you and the neighboring children who have words and fight; someone gets a black eye; but you make up and then you work and play together again and as you grow more mature you fight less often because you become more intelligent. So will it be with the world "

In giving these simple facts to my children I continually add to my own faith in mankind. I believe man is basically good in heart, spiritually indestructible, and his place in the sun is assured because he is in God's image. I believe all these things sincerely—but more important—my children believe them, for it is they who hold the combination to man's future peace and happiness.

H LLOYD JORDAN, a much-decorated bomber group commander in the Second World War, is now a pilot for Eastern Air Lines He married his boyhood sweetheart They live with their three children on a picturesque island off the Florida coast, in the midst of an old coconut plantation.

Mr. Jordan is an ardent sportsman, his favorite pastimes being golf, waterskiing, and spearfishing This latter sport takes him out to the outer reefs close to the Gulf Stream, where he dives to eerie depths. He tells many thrilling stories of personal encounters with sharks, barracudas, and even with such a thing as an occasional sunken treasure ship.

In his profession, he meets people from all parts of the country and in all walks of life. As a result of these contacts, he believes that his choice of occupation and close-to-nature way of living have made the Jordans, in his words, "the most successfully happy family I have ever known "

The Light of a Brighter Day

BY HELEN KELLER

I CHOOSE for my subject faith wrought into life, apart from creed or dogma. By faith I mean a vision of good one cherishes and the enthusiasm that pushes one to seek its fulfillment regardless of obstacles. Faith is a dynamic power that breaks the chain of routine and gives a new, fine turn to old commonplaces. Faith reinvigorates the will, enriches the affections and awakens a sense of creativeness.

Active faith knows no fear, and it is a safeguard to me against cynicism and despair. After all, faith is not one thing or two or three things; it is an indivisible totality of beliefs that inspire me Belief in God as infinite good will and all-seeing Wisdom whose everlasting arms sustain me walking on the sea of life. Trust in my fellow men, wonder at their fundamental goodness and confidence that after this night of sorrow and oppression they will rise up strong and beautiful in the glory of morning. Reverence for the beauty and preciousness of earth, and a sense of responsibility to do what I can to make it a habitation of health and plenty for all men. Faith in immortality because it renders less bitter the separation from those I have loved and lost, and because it will free me from unnatural limitations and unfold still more faculties I have in joyous activity. Even if my vital spark should be blown out, I believe that I should behave with courageous dignity in the presence of fate and strive to be a worthy companion of the Beautiful, the Good and the True But fate has its master in the faith of those who surmount it, and limitation has its limits for those who, though disillusioned, live greatly. True faith is not a fruit of security, it is the ability to blend mortal fragility with the inner strength of the spirit. It does not shift with the changing shades of one's thought.

It was a terrible blow to my faith when I learned that millions of my fellow creatures must labor all their days for food and shelter, bear the most crushing burdens and die without having known the

89

joy of living. My security vanished forever, and I have never regained the radiant belief of my young years that earth is a happy home and hearth for the majority of mankind. But faith is a state of mind. The believer is not soon disheartened. If he is turned out of his shelter, he builds up a house that the winds of the earth cannot destroy.

When I think of the suffering and famine, and the continued slaughter of men, my spirit bleeds, but the thought comes to me that, like the little deaf, dumb and blind child I once was, mankind is growing out of the darkness of ignorance and hate into the light of a brighter day.

HELEN KELLER has been blind and deaf since she was nineteen months old. By slow stages she painfully learned to appreciate a world more fortunate people take for granted. Aided by her friend and teacher, the late Anne Sullivan Macy, she was able to sharpen her other senses to the point where they help compensate for her loss of sight and hearing. Thus she was able to gain an education and graduated from Radcliffe College cum laude in 1904.

Even before that she had begun to write, and her autobiography, *The Story of My Life*, was published in the *Ladies' Home Journal* Since then she has written steadily. Her numerous books include *The World I Live In*.

When she is not traveling, this remarkable woman, now in her seventies, lives in a white frame house in Westport, Connecticut, with Polly Thomson. For nearly forty years, Miss Thomson has been her constant companion and has helped her emerge from a blind and deaf-mute's prison to communicate so richly with the world.

Matisse and the Music of Discontent

BY ANDRE KOSTELANETZ

ON EASTER SUNDAY, 1945, the last year of the war, my wife and I were in Marseilles. We had just arrived for four days rest, after a tour of entertaining the troops in Burma It was a wonderful morning, sparkling but not too warm, there were no tourists of course, and we decided to drive along the Riviera to Vence and call on Matisse. We had never met the painter, but we knew well his son Pierre in New York.

We found Matisse living in a small house, with a magnificent, sweeping view beyond his vegetable garden. In one room there was a cage with a lot of fluttering birds. The place was covered with paintings, most of them obviously new ones. I marveled at his production and I asked him, "What is your inspiration?"

"I grow artichokes," he said. His eyes smiled at my surprise and he went on to explain: "Every morning I go into the garden and watch these plants. I see the play of light and shade on the leaves and I discover new combinations of colors and fantastic patterns. I study them. They inspire me. Then I go back into the studio and paint"

This struck me forcefully. Here was perhaps the world's most celebrated living painter. He was approaching eighty and I would have thought that he had seen every combination of light and shade imaginable. Yet every day he got fresh inspiration from the sunlight on an artichoke; it seemed to charge the delicate dynamo of his genius with an effervescent energy almost inexhaustible.

I wondered what might have happened if Matisse had never taken that morning stroll in the garden. But such a withdrawal is not in his character. Sometimes a man builds a wall around himself, shutting out the light. Not Matisse. He goes out to meet the world, discovers it and seems to soak up the discoveries in his very pores.

In such a process, man inhales the chemicals of inspiration, so to

91

speak. As a musician, inspiration is vital to me but I find it hard to define what it is. It is more than just drinking in a view or being in love. It is, I think, a sense of discovery, a keen appetite for something new. There goes with it a certain amount of discipline, of control, coupled with a reluctance to accept a rigid, preconceived pattern Someone has described this whole feeling as a divine discontent.

The source of this capacity for thrilling, explanatory wonder at life rests, I believe, above man himself in something supreme. I sense this in regarding nature, which stimulates me in all my creative work. There are a host of things about the universe which I do not clearly understand, any more than I can understand, for example, the technicalities of the process by which we can be heard and seen in this new dimension, the miraculous television screen. Such finite things as these inventions were inconceivable mysteries a few years ago. The reason for life may be obscure to me, but that is no cause to doubt that the reason is there. Like Matisse with his artichoke, I can regard the infinite number of lights and shades of a piece of music and know that this is true.

◦§ ANDRE KOSTELANETZ is a name that means many things to many people To a vast audience in many lands, he is the most listened-to conductor on phonograph records. To veterans of World War II, he was the man who organized and conducted "GI" orchestras on every fighting front from Germany to the Pacific. To concert-goers everywhere he is one of the most popular conductors ever to lead such orchestras as the New York Philharmonic, the Philadelphia Orchestra and the Boston Symphony

Above all he is revered by contemporary American composers as a champion who has labored constantly to bring their works before the musical world. His enthusiasm and foresight led him to commission many compositions which have now taken their place in the standard American repertoire

A man of enormous vitality, with blue eyes which can be laughing and piercing at the same time, his interests are manifold Literature and art, philosophy and sports all fascinate him But music has always come first with this Russian-born maestro.

I Beseech You to Look

BY OLGA KOUSSEVITZKY

I CANNOT SPEAK of my belief without also speaking of my innermost personal and spiritual experiences. As certain landmarks determine the course we take in life, so, too, our experiences leave an imprint upon our souls and beliefs.

I shall briefly recall two outstanding experiences in my life. First, as a very young girl, after a happy cloudless childhood, I entered a world charged with tempest and trials. a world war, a revolution, a civil war, famine, flight and exile. . . . It was nevertheless during those trying years that I came closer to perceiving the truth of faith and the light of the Grace of God which transcends all understanding and shines in the midst of the "darkness at noon." As Fra Giovanni said in the turbulent sixteenth century. "There is radiance and glory in darkness, could we but see: and to see, we have only to look. I beseech you to look. . . ."

It is my firm belief that, even as the malignant growth of evil threatens, confuses, attacks and spreads in the world, the light of grace is active through the innocent, the persecuted, the humble and the oppressed. It is present in our midst today.

My other experience, in later years, was deeply rewarding and illuminating. To have been near Serge Koussevitzky and not take fire from his flame, ideals and beliefs would have been well-nigh impossible His was an all-consuming flame and belief in music. His apostolic fervor gave him an almost superhuman power of communication and endurance Each musical performance was to him a new and supreme offering.

It was his presence and his flaming spirit that helped to mold and shape my innermost thought, and to accept life in its unyielding stride and unending inspiration. When his life departed and the light went out of my life, I was given to experience the glow and warmth of heart of those who loved and admired my husband. I saw the path he lighted to those of us who were close to him—his associates, his pupils. For me and for mankind, Serge Koussevitzky left a spiritual heritage, in the dedication of his life and the light of his art, for he was truly an artist by the Grace of God.

OLGA KOUSSEVITZKY was born on the Volga estate of her family in pre-revolutionary Russia. When she was twelve, she attended her first musical performance, a symphony concert by her uncle-by-marriage, Serge Koussevitzky, little realizing how much he would someday mean to her Her traditional family life came to a sudden end with the Revolution in 1917.

Her father, Alexander Naoumoff, prominent in government circles in Tsarist Russia (his memoirs are preserved in the Hoover War Library at Stanford University), escaped with his family in 1920 Fleeing by way of Constantinople and Greece, they sought refuge in France In 1929 she accompanied Mr. and Mrs. Koussevitzky to America as their secretary

When her aunt Natalie died in 1942, Olga shared the deep grief of Serge Koussevitzky. Five years later they were quietly married in his Lenox home, not to part again until the death of the famed conductor in 1951.

John Donne Was Right

BY DR. MAX T. KRONE

SOMETIME AGO I saw an electron microscope photograph of a slice of tissue from the brain of a mouse. The brain cells of this mouse had been cut so thin that it would have taken five hundred thousand such slices to make a pile an inch high.

The brain cells themselves had been enlarged so many times by the microscope that had the tiny mouse who gave his life for this scientific experiment been enlarged proportionately he would have assumed the dimensions of some prehistoric dinosaur. Truly I was having a view of life so close to my eyes that there was not space to blink.

Just recently I saw another photograph, one taken through the two-hundred-inch telescope at Palomar of a star so far away from us that its light had taken some fabulous number of light years—was it billions or trillions?—to reach that sensitized photographic plate even though it was traveling 186,000 miles a second. My vision had been extended both into the past and into space . . . so far that I could only marvel breathlessly at the sweep of infinity that lay behind and around me.

As I have thought of these two photographs I have wondered if by chance there were some being on that distant star whose intelligence had so surpassed ours that he had been able to develop instruments so much more sensitive than ours that he could not only see the little ball we call the earth, revolving out in space, but that he might also be able to see those tiny specks called men that creep and fly about this ball. And what if he might also be able to hear the things we say or even hear the things we think! What would he think of these men?

What would I think of myself if I had such a place in space and time from which I might observe my actions, scan my thoughts and hear the things I say? What would I then leave unsaid, and what undone?

I believe that could I reflect upon the life I watch myself unfold from such a distant star, I would not be content or happy unless I had worked to leave that little part of the world in which I had lived some tiny bit better a place in which to live than it was when I was born into it.

Just what form and direction my life would take with such compulsion would depend upon many things—upon the particular part of the world of which I was a part and the people with whom my lot was cast. It would depend upon the particular combination of cells that formed my brain and body and which laid down the pattern of interests and abilities that were mine.

But this I believe: that from such a vantage point in time and space I would see the truth that John Donne saw when he wrote, "No man is an island." And I am sure I would see that man, of all the forms of life that inhabit this revolving ball, the earth, has been given a unique capacity for enjoying it. But he has also inherited an infinite capacity for creating misery, unhappiness, both within himself and in his fellow men. And I believe I would see—far off in space and time— that the two are closely related, that I cannot be truly happy while my fellow man is miserable, oppressed, sick in mind and body, hungry, cold, unclothed, unenlightened, and unable to enjoy the beauty in the world about him. For I would see from afar what I too often cannot see at close quarters—that "earth is fair and all her folk be one."

◄§ MAX T. KRONE left his native Pennsylvania and, taking Horace Greeley's advice, went west—by degrees. Schooled in Ohio, he attended the University of Illinois and received his doctorate from Northwestern University After teaching at Illinois, Northwestern, and Western Reserve, he went on to the University of California, where he is now Dean of the Institute of the Arts

Nationally known as a choral director, he is the author of various works on choral music With his wife, Beatrice Perham Krone, he has produced more than three hundred arrangements of folk music. Founder-director of the Idyllwild Arts Foundation, he believes that an education based upon the arts is a universal means of understanding among all peoples.

The twinkle in his blue eyes reveals both his sense of humor and his quick sensitivity, coupled with these qualities is a strength of will evidenced in his administrative leadership

Inspiration from a Drainpipe

BY MRS. JOHN G. LEE

I THINK the most profound influence in my life was my father. He was an inventor and a scientist with a most inquisitive mind He loved and was greatly stimulated by the beauty and the design he found in nature. He believed in people and was himself a completely honest person. His sense of humor was keen though kindly and his energy was inexhaustible. Once he was asked how he got the idea for the Maxim Silencer. He answered, "By watching the way water behaved when it went down a drain." This simple statement opened up for me a whole realm of ideas which led to a firm belief that human intelligence need recognize no bounds; that through the use of our intelligence we will move progressively closer to an understanding of man and of the universe around us; that this knowledge will bring a closer harmony between man and his surroundings; and that this way lies the chance to make the world a better place to live in.

Then I remember sitting with him on the deck of his boat one night in early September We were anchored in a secluded cove The breeze was light and very salty We could hear across a little strip of land the pounding of the surf. The stars were brilliant and every now and then a shooting star would streak across the sky. He was deeply interested in astronomy and he led my mind into unforgettable speculation as we explored the grandeur of that night. I think from this I came to understand that there must be law and order in our universe There is design Man can observe, he can learn to understand, he can apply. The secret is to apply in the interests of the common good; not for one or for a few; not to destroy but to build for all peoples.

My mother and father each had an acute social conscience. They believed that because good fortune had endowed them with better than average opportunity, they had a duty to perform in their communities. From this no doubt came my own conviction that I must give more than I receive and that a satisfactory life must be measured by its usefulness to others.

I remember the excitement engendered by the conversation in our home. All kinds of ideas were explored; all sorts of prejudices were challenged; penetrating minds were brought to bear on every problem of the day. I learned that each one of us has a right to his own beliefs, that prejudice perverts truth and that violence in the long run gains us nothing. From this understanding I moved into the belief that people everywhere must learn how to work together for the common purpose of the betterment of mankind.

I believe one of the greatest ideas of all times, one that is a compelling moral force, is the concept of the dignity and worth of the human individual. From this idea there develops a sense of devotion to the common good.

I believe that if we pull these rather simple but fundamental things together and tie them up with honesty and truth, there are no visible limits to the heights to which mankind can rise.

◄§ MRS. JOHN G LEE, a trim-figured, curly-haired mother of four and youngish-looking grandmother of two, commutes nearly every week from her home in Farmington, Connecticut, to her work in Washington She is President of the League of Women Voters of the United States

Her husband, an aeronautical engineer who specializes in military aviation, completely agrees with Mrs. Lee that someone in the family should concentrate on more strictly peaceful pursuits. Now with many years of work in the League behind her, she heads the national organization of 106,000 women who work in 848 communities to encourage more citizens to take an active interest in the affairs of government.

Mrs. Lee passed up college to marry at nineteen and raise a family When she is not working twelve to eighteen hours a day in Washington, she spends her time sailing and riding with her family.

The Only Way to Make a Friend

BY HERBERT H. LEHMAN

So MANY THINGS affect a man's philosophy and his life that I find it difficult to put into words my personal beliefs. I hesitate to speak of them publicly for fear of giving the appearance of preaching.

Two convictions, however, I believe have more than any others influenced my thinking both in private and in public life.

First, commonplace as it may sound, I am convinced that what we get out of life is in direct proportion to what we put into it. Second, I must respect the opinions of others even if I disagree with them.

Throughout my long and rather busy career I have always held firmly to the belief that I owe life as much as it owes to me. If that philosophy is sound, and I believe it is, it applies, I hope, to all of my activities—to my home, to my daily work, to my politics, and above all things to my relationships to others

Life is not a one-way street. What I do, what I say, even what I think, inevitably has a direct effect on my relationships with others. I am certain that in the degree that my attitude towards others has given convincing proof of loyalty, sincerity, honesty, courtesy and fairness, I have encouraged in others the same attitude towards me. Respect begets respect, suspicion begets suspicion, hate begets hate. It has been well said that "The only way to have a friend is to be one."

None of the blessings of our great American heritage of civil liberties is self-executing. To make effective such things as brotherhood, kindliness, sympathy, human decency, the freedom of opportunity, the very preciousness of life—to make these things real requires respect and constant vigilance. This is the core of my American Faith.

As I have said, I believe I must help to safeguard to all men free expression of their views even though I may be in disagreement with them. I must listen to and study *responsible* views; sometimes I will learn much from them. No individual and no nation has a monopoly

99

of wisdom or talent. When an individual or a nation becomes self-satisfied or complacent, it is time, I believe, to be deeply concerned. He who closes his ears to the views of others shows little confidence in the integrity of his own views.

There can be no question with regard to the inherent rights of Americans to enjoy equal economic opportunity in every field, to secure decent living conditions, adequate provision for the moral and spiritual development of their children, and free association with their fellow men as equals under the law and equals in the sight of God These rights can be safeguarded and advanced only where men may think and speak freely. I reject a fundamental principle of democracy if I seek to prevent a fellow citizen of different background from fully expressing his thoughts on any subject I have tried to express a few of my own thoughts on this subject which is very close to me I think that we will have good reason for optimism about the future of the American ideal as long as men can and will say, without fear, what they believe.

§ HERBERT H. LEHMAN has had a long and distinguished career in business and public life. For thirty years after his graduation from Williams College in 1899 he engaged in commercial, industrial, and banking activities. In 1928 he was elected Lieutenant Governor of New York, serving for four years. He was elected Governor and served ten years.

In 1943 he was chosen Director General of the United Nations Relief and Rehabilitation Administration by the unanimous vote of forty-four nations. This organization dispensed over three and a half billion dollars and saved millions of people from starvation Decorated by many foreign governments for his services to humanity, he also holds the Distinguished Service Medal

In 1949 he was elected United States Senator from New York to fill the unexpired term of Senator Robert F Wagner, and in 1950 was re-elected for a full six-year term.

I Wish I Could Believe

BY C. DAY LEWIS

"The best lack all conviction,
While the worst are full of passionate intensity."

THOSE TWO LINES of Yeats for me sum up the matter as it stands today when the very currency of belief seems debased. I was brought up in the Christian church. Later I believed for a while that communism offered the best hope for this world. I acknowledge the need for belief, but I cannot forget how through the ages great faiths have been vitiated by fanaticism and dogmatism, by intolerance and cruelty, by the intellectual dishonesty, the folly, the crankiness or the opportunism of their adherents.

Have I no faith at all, then? Faith is the thing at the core of you, the sediment that's left when hopes and illusions are drained away. The thing for which you make any sacrifice because without it you would be nothing—a mere walking shadow. I know what my own core is. I would in the last resort sacrifice any human relationship, any way of living to the search for truth which produces my poem. I know there are heavy odds against any poem I write surviving after my death I realize that writing poetry may seem the most preposterously useless thing a man can be doing today. Yet it is just at such times of crisis that each man discovers or rediscovers what he values most. My poet's instinct to make something comes out most strongly then, enabling me to use fear, doubt, even despair as creative stimuli. In doing so, I feel my kinship with humanity, with the common man who carries on doing his job till the bomb falls or the sea closes over him. Carries on because of his belief, however inarticulate, that this is the best thing he can do. But the poet is luckier than the layman, for his job is always a vocation. Indeed, it's so like a religious vocation that he may feel little need for a religious faith, but because it is always trying to get past the trivial and the transient or to reveal these as images of the essential and the permanent, poetry is at least a kind of spiritual activity.

Men need a religious belief to make sense out of life. I wish I had such a belief myself, but any creed of mine would be honeycombed with confusions and reservations Yet when I write a poem I am trying to make sense out of life. And just now and then my experience composes and transmutes itself into a poem which tells me something I didn't know I knew. So for me the compulsion of poetry is the sign of a belief, not the less real for being unformulated . . . a belief that men must enjoy life, explore life, enhance life. Each as best he can. And that I shall do these things best through the practice of poetry.

C DAY LEWIS is one of Britain's leading poets and was awarded the C B E. in the 1950 Birthday Honours List He was educated at Sherborne School and at Wadham College, Oxford While at the University, he met Stephen Spender and W. H Auden, the latter having a profound influence on Mr. Lewis' early poetry.

He soon became a widely respected poet in his own right. In a preface to a selection of his poems he says, "We write in order to understand, not in order to be understood; though the more successfully a poem has interpreted to its writer the meaning of his experience, the more widely will it be 'understood' in the long run."

In 1951 Mr. Lewis was elected to the Chair of Poetry at Oxford He frequently broadcasts readings of poetry for the BBC, sometimes with his wife, Jill Balcon Under the pseudonym of Nicholas Blake he has written detective stories. His poetry is represented in most anthologies of modern verse.

Diogenes Didn't Need a Lamp

BY DAVID LOTH

I BELIEVE in people. However much of a mess we seem to make of the world, it is people who have brought about all the progress we know, and I don't mean just material progress. All have been formulated and expressed by men and women. Even when people make mistakes it seems to me they usually make them from right motives. Most of us want to do good.

I believe in people because I have seen a great many of them in different parts of the world. I would rather trust my own experience and observation than the cynical remarks of unhappy men. My belief not only has given me a happy life but has made possible any really useful work I have done.

Of course I like people, too. As a newspaperman for twenty years in this country, Europe and Australia, I met all kinds of men and women and saw them under both favorable and adverse conditions. As a biographer, I learned that the people of other days were not much different than we are today. The lesson of history, both the history of the past and the history we are making on this particular day of today, is that the people's instincts are almost always right. You can trust them. Their information may be wrong and their thinking muddled, but their feelings are sound, and progress stems from this fact.

I lived in Spain at the time of the overthrow of the monarchy in 1931, and first heard of the establishment of a new republic when our cook came from the market, breathless with the news. Her very first comment, expressing what was uppermost in her mind, was given with an almost exalted look: "Señor, now our children will learn to read and write."

It was a wonderful thing to see people animated by these ideals, carrying out a bloodless revolution. I remember a dance at which the lights were turned out during the playing of the new republican anthem "because," as one republic leader told me, "this is a social affair and we don't want to see who won't stand up " That the counterrevolution was cruel and bitter does not change the fact that the people themselves in those years of progress were gentle and tolerant.

I know nothing that proves the spirit of divinity in human beings more than the press's preoccupation with evil. As a newspaperman myself, I always preferred digging into stories of violence or crime or betrayal because they were so unusual. I once wrote a history of political corruption in America, and after years of research I had to base it on fewer than one per cent of our public servants Searching for crooks brought me into contact—historically speaking—with many more honest men. I hardly mentioned them in the book, but they are much more important to me than the grafters. On the day that I find myself being surprised by evidences of loyalty and integrity and tolerance in my fellow men, then I will have lost my faith.

DAVID LOTH is the author of ten volumes of biography and history and co-author or "ghost" of ten other books, chiefly on health and family living. This ambitious sweep complemented itself, he points out, since a biography requires knowledge of the subject's health and domestic life as well as of his achievements and career.

As a newspaperman, Mr Loth spent ten years on the staff of the old New York World and seven with The New York Times. In between he was editor and publisher of Spain's first English periodical. During World War II he served as Chief of Publications of the Office of Inter-American Affairs and Director of Information for the Surplus Property Board.

An insatiable interest in people has been responsible for his travels and his books, he says He now lives in the Hudson valley, not far above New York City, where he combines writing with "extremely amateur gardening and middle-aged tennis."

Three O' Cat Is Still Game

BY LILLIAN BUENO McCUE

WHAT DO I BELIEVE? What laws do I live by? There are so many answers—work, beauty, truth, love—and I hope I do live by them.

But in everyday things I live by the light of a supplementary set of laws. I'd better call them rules of thumb. Rules of thumb aren't very grand, but they do make the wheels go round.

My father and mother sent me to good schools, but the finest thing they did for my education was to have seven children. I was the oldest, and my brothers and sisters were my best teachers.

I learned first to pull my own weight in the boat. Kids making a bob-sled have no use for the loafer who wants a free ride. Neither has the world. I learned to make the bed I slept in, and wash the glass I used, and mend what I broke, and mop up where I spilled. And if I was too lazy or too dainty or too busy, and left it for someone else, somebody else soon taught me different.

Then, the same way, I learned that anger is a waste. It hurts nobody but me. A fit of the sullens got short shrift in our house. It wasn't pulling my weight in the boat. It was spoiling sport. And among seven children it got me nowhere. It might reduce four o' cat to three o' cat, but the game went on just the same, and where was I? Out of it. Better go in and join the group around the piano and forget my grievance. Better still, next time don't fling down my bat in a tantrum; keep my temper, and stay in the game.

Here's a rule of thumb that's important, and the older I get, the more important I think it is When I can do something, and somebody wants me to do it, I have to do it. The great tragedy of life is not to be needed. As long as you are able and willing to do things for people, you will be needed. Of course you are able, and if so, you can't say no My mother is seventy-seven. In seventy-seven years she has never said no. Today she is so much in demand by thirteen grandchildren and countless neighbors that her presence is eagerly contended for. When I want to see her I have to pretend emergency.

Then there's the rule of curiosity. Your body would die if you stopped feeling hunger and thirst, and your mind will die if you lose your curiosity. This I learned from my father. My father was a naturalist. He could see the beetle under the bark, and draw it forth unharmed for us to squint at through the magnifying glass He sampled the taste of thirty-three different caterpillars Fired by his example, once, my sister ate an ant In case you are wondering, caterpillars taste like the green leaves they eat, and ants taste of lemon. I personally haven't tasted any entomological specimens lately, but I am still rejoicing in the limitless curiosity that draws me to books and people and places. I hope I never lose it. It would be like pulling down the blind.

Finally, there is the rule of happiness. Happiness is a habit. I was taught to cultivate it. A big stomach-ache, or a big heart-ache, can interrupt happiness, but neither can destroy it unless I permit. My mother simply wouldn't have unhappy faces moping about the place. If it was stomach-ache, she dosed it. If it was heart-ache, she administered love and understanding and lots of interesting things to do, and soon the sun came out again. Even the heartbreaks that can't really be mended, even those seem to yield to the habit of finding happiness in doing things, in love and in the memory of love. I hope I never lose that habit either. It would be like putting out the light.

So I learned to live, by the great laws, and these little rules of thumb. I wouldn't take a million dollars for any one of them, or a million times that for the years at home that taught them to me.

LILLIAN B MC CUE has written several books under the pen name of Lillian de la Torre. She was born in New York in 1902, and holds degrees from the College of New Rochelle, Columbia and Radcliffe, and has studied at the University of Munich

After half a lifetime spent in what she calls "tinkering with words," Mrs. McCue began to write in earnest A special interest in history, particularly the eighteenth century, combined with a love of detective fiction to provide her with a field of literary operation— the "solving" of famous mysteries. Her books in this vein include *Elizabeth Is Missing, Dr Sam Johnson, Detector,* and *The Heir of Douglas.*

A physically big woman, she enjoys life and people. She likes to cook and has written *The 60-Minute Chef,* enjoys amateur theatricals and travel She and her husband, a professor of English, live in Colorado Springs.

The Vital Human Difference

BY RICHARD H. McFEELY

I HAVE always loved sports. In high school and college I played almost everything—football, basketball, baseball, lacrosse, and all the rest. I had planned graduate study in physical education and then working in it with young people. Suddenly, during the football season in my senior year in college, I was stricken with infantile paralysis. I was told I had lost the use of my legs forever except with crutches or braces.

Two of the most valuable lessons of my life grew out of this crippling attack. At first I was very low in mind and spirit. I had no real hope for the future. One day my mother revealed to me the two lessons which have helped me immeasurably ever since. She realized, as only a mother can, the depths of my mental depression. She wanted to help me by giving me something that would sustain me, strengthen a waning courage, revitalize a spirit of self-forgetfulness.

"Dick," she said, "what life does to you in the long run will depend on what life finds in you. You know we can change any situation by changing our own attitudes toward it." She went on to point out that we could not always explain our hard luck, which so often seemed unjust and undeserved.

"Remember," she added, "it is not so much what life brings to us in her hands as what we bring to life in our spirits—this makes the real difference between persons."

The other point Mother developed for me was this. "No one ever finds life worth living One always has to make it worth living. Look at all the men and women who have lived successful, creative lives —in whatever period of history. They have not always been the prosperous, the fortunate, sitting on the cushioned seats. . . . Look at Jesus, poor, homeless, misunderstood, crucified. Beethoven," she went on, "created some of his greatest music after he was deaf. Helen Keller and other moderns have also risen above life's adversities and

107

misfortunes. They did so in spite of such circumstances and because of the courageous spirit within them."

Remembering this advice in the intervening years, I have asked myself, "Is life worth living?" and I have found the answer in the attitudes we hold and the quality of our spirit, not outward circumstances. Birth and death, happiness and sorrow, illness and good health, love and loss—these I find are no respecters of persons. They come alike to all. But not all respond alike. Some go to pieces, dissolve in self-pity, become a burden to others, perhaps even take their own lives in their despair and hopelessness. Others have something in them that in spite of ill fortune enables them to live constructively and creatively. Ofttimes it is more difficult to live a happy, useful life when all the breaks seem to be good ones.

For the most part, I think that what all things do to us will depend on what they find in us. "Life does not consist in holding a good hand, but in playing a bad hand well."

Together with these thoughts inspired by my mother in a dark hour of my life, I have long found help and inspiration in this prayer by Charles Lewis Slattery:

"Almighty God, we thank thee for the job of this day: may we find gladness in all its toil and difficulty, in its pleasure and success, and even in its failure and sorrow. We would look always away from ourselves, and behold the glory and the need of the world that we may have the will and the strength to bring the gift of gladness to others; that with them we may stand to bear the burden and heat of the day and offer thee the praise of work well done. Amen."

◄§ RICHARD H. MC FEELY was stricken with infantile paralysis while he was a football-playing student at Swarthmore College in 1927. Recuperating at Warm Springs, Georgia, he formed a friendship with another man who also had to build a new life, Franklin D Roosevelt. By 1929 he had sufficiently recovered to allow him to become assistant dean of men at Swarthmore.

For the next fifteen years he was on the faculty of George School in Bucks County, Pennsylvania. From 1945 until 1949, when he returned to George School to become headmaster, he was headmaster of Friends Central School in the Overbrook section of Philadelphia. Whenever he has free time from his duties as school head and as a highly popular speaker, he likes to play his accordion and to follow sports.

The Strange and Wonderful Thing

BY DR. ROBERT M. MacIVER

WHEN I was a boy a stone was to me a stone, and that was a bit of worn-down rock that could be kicked about or thrown at things. And earth was earth, and that was an inert crumbly stuff in which things crawled and grew. Everything was what it was. Things were just what our sense said they were.

I learned in time that the stone had a strange history over millions of years. I learned that mighty forces had formed and baked it, buried it and smoothed it Then I learned that the dead stone was composed of infinitesimal atoms.

I learned that the inconceivably small atom was itself a system and that its constituents whirled in their orbits with incredible swiftness.

In short, everything turned out to be more and more different from what it seemed to be. It was my ignorance that made me think things common and ordinary, for they are strange and wonderful.

What has all this to do with beliefs? It certainly has a lot to do with mine. Let me draw a moral or two which may explain what I mean. One is that in learning about things we never learn the causes of things. We learn more about things, and the things change amazingly as we learn, but we never learn to explain their being

We discover the atom and it becomes another form of energy. But what is energy? And if someday energy turns out to be something else again we are no nearer to explaining it than before.

My beliefs furnish no answer to many of my questions. They do not tell me what immortality means, as imputed to personal existence, what it could mean or whether it has any meaning. They tell me that only what has been from the first is immortal, but what was first and in what manner of being is beyond my grasp. I believe that everything belongs forever with all things, but how it belongs and will belong I can't comprehend.

What we have in common with all, what we share and do not diminish by sharing, the common pulse, the common life, the common destiny, holds what is richest and deepest in ourselves, and in the sympathetic understanding of it lies first whatever of divinity we can attain.

A seventeenth-century thinker, Sir Thomas Browne, said he loved to pursue his thoughts to a point where he had to stop and cry: "Oh, the far heights!" That is about all I can do. The wonder is in me and encompasses me and lies forever beyond—and, knowing no name for it, I call it God.

◆§ DR. ROBERT M. MAC IVER, professor emeritus of political philosophy and sociology at Columbia University, was born in Stornoway, Scotland. This lean, white-haired teacher still speaks with a musical Scottish accent which has been only slightly tempered by his long residence in Canada and this country

With earned degrees from Edinburgh University and Oxford, and honorary ones from Harvard and Columbia Universities, he has lectured on political science at Aberdeen University in Scotland, at the University of Toronto, and at Barnard College His international honors include a Fellowship in the Royal Society of Canada.

Dr. MacIver's many published works include The Web of Government and The More Perfect Union. His home is in Palisades, New York, but he summers in Martha's Vineyard. When not engaged in scholarly work, he likes to play the piano, is especially fond of Gilbert and Sullivan, and is noted for being an expert on mushrooms.

Twice I Sought Death

BY MRS. MARTY MANN

I AM AN ALCOHOLIC—one of the fortunate ones who found the road to recovery. That was thirteen years ago, but I haven't forgotten. I remember what it was like to be hopelessly in the grip of the vicious disease of alcoholism, not knowing what was wrong with me. I remember my desperate search for help Failing to find it, I remember my inner despair—my outer defiance.

I remember the arrogance and pride with which I faced the non-understanding world, in spite of my terrible hidden fears—my fear of life and my fear of death. At times I feared life so much more than death that twice I sought death. Suicide seemed a welcome release from a terror and agony past bearing.

How grateful I am now that I didn't succeed. But I believed in nothing, then. Not in myself, nor in anything outside myself. I was walled in with my suffering—alone and, I thought, forsaken.

But I wasn't forsaken, of course. No one is, really I seemed to suffer alone, but I believe now that I was never alone—that none of us are. I believe, too, that I was never given more to bear than I could endure, but rather that my suffering was necessary, for me. I believe it may well have taken that much suffering, in my case, to break down my wall of self, to crush my arrogance and pride, to let me seek and accept the help that was there.

For in the depths of my suffering I came to believe. To believe that there was a Power greater than myself that could help me. To believe that because of that Power—God—there was hope and help for me

I found my help through people—doctors whose vocation it is to deal with suffering, and other human beings who had suffered like myself. In the depths of my personal abyss I received understanding and kindness and help from many individuals People, I learned, can be very kind. I came to believe deeply in this—in people and the good that is in them.

I came to realize that suffering is universal. It lies behind much apparent harshness and irritability, many of the careless, even cruel, words and acts which make our daily lives difficult so much of the time. I learned that if I could understand this, I might not react so often with anger or hurt. And if I learned to react to difficult behavior with understanding and sympathy, I might help to bring about a change in that behavior. My suffering helped me to know things.

I do not believe that everyone *should* suffer. But I do believe that suffering can be good, and even necessary, *if*—and only if—one learns to accept that suffering as part of one's essential learning process, and then to use it to help oneself and one's fellow sufferers.

Don't we all endure suffering, one way or another? This fact gives me a deep sense of kinship with other people and a consequent desire to help others in any and every way I can.

It is this belief that underlies my work, for alcoholism is the area in which I feel best fitted, through my own experience, to help others. And I believe that trying to help my fellow men is one of the straightest roads to spiritual growth. It is a road everyone can take. One doesn't have to be beautiful or gifted, or rich or powerful, in order to offer a helping hand to one's fellow sufferers. And I believe that one can walk with God by doing just that.

◄§ MRS MARTY MANN is executive director of the National Committee on Alcoholism The daughter of an executive of Marshall Field's Chicago department store, she returned from a European education in 1926 to find America in the midst of Prohibition. Not realizing that alcohol was physically dangerous to her, she fell into the fashionable habit of visiting speakeasies. The affliction became worse and she had to give up a promising career After her recovery at Blythewood Sanitarium she became the first woman member of Alcoholics Anonymous.

In 1944 she helped found the National Committee on Alcoholism in association with Yale University. The primary function of this group is to change public opinion regarding alcoholism and to establish a program for its treatment. Their basic premise is that alcoholism is a disease and must be treated as such

Graying, stylish Mrs. Mann is fond of the theater and the ballet. For recreation she enjoys reading and music as well as swimming and riding.

Life Grows in the Soil of Time

BY THOMAS MANN

WHAT I BELIEVE, what I value most, is transitoriness.

But is not transitoriness—the perishableness of life—something very sad? No! It is the very soul of existence It imparts value, dignity, interest to life. Transitoriness creates time—and "time is the essence." Potentially at least, time is the supreme, most useful gift.

Time is related to—yes, identical with—everything creative and active, every progress toward a higher goal.

Without transitoriness, without beginning or end, birth or death, there is no time, either. Timelessness—in the sense of time never ending, never beginning—is a stagnant nothing. It is absolutely uninteresting.

Life is possessed by tremendous tenacity. Even so its presence remains conditional, and as it had a beginning, so it will have an end. I believe that life, just for this reason, is exceedingly enhanced in value, in charm.

One of the most important characteristics distinguishing man from all other forms of nature is his knowledge of transitoriness, of beginning and end, and therefore of the gift of time.

In man transitory life attains its peak of animation, of soul power, so to speak. This does not mean man alone would have a soul. Soul quality pervades all beings. But man's soul is most awake in his knowledge of the interchangeability of the terms "existence" and "transitoriness."

To man time is given like a piece of land, as it were, entrusted to him for faithful tilling, a space in which to strive incessantly, achieve self-realization, move onward and upward. Yes, with the aid of time, man becomes capable of wresting the immortal from the mortal.

Deep down, I believe—and deem such belief natural to every human soul—that in the universe prime significance must be attributed to this earth of ours. Deep down I believe that creation of

113

the universe out of nothingness and of life out of inorganic state ultimately aimed at the creation of man. I believe that man is meant as a great experiment whose possible failure of man's own guilt would be paramount to the failure of creation itself.

Whether this belief be true or not, man would be well advised if he behaved as though it were.

THOMAS MANN, the novelist, has been variously referred to as "the last great European" and "the heir of Goethe" He was born in Lubeck, Germany, of an old and influential mercantile family He showed his genius at an early age. Buddenbrooks, published while he was still in his middle twenties, made him a world figure. More than a million copies of this classic were sold in pre-Hitler Germany.

In 1927 he published his second great novel, The Magic Mountain, which consolidated his reputation. In 1929 he received the Nobel Prize for Literature and in 1937 the Cardinal Newman Award A militant anti-Fascist, he was forced to leave his country and was deprived of his citizenship He settled in America.

Another famous work, Joseph and His Brothers, has been hailed as one of the masterpieces of all time Dr Mann now lives and works in Santa Monica, California. He has three sons and three daughters.

A New Control of Destiny

BY MARGARET MEAD

CHILDREN USED TO PLAY a game of pointing at someone suddenly, saying: "What are you?" Some people answered by saying: "I am a human being," or by nationality, or by religion. When this question was put to me by a new generation of children, I answered: "An anthropologist." Anthropology is the study of whole ways of life, to which one must be completely committed, all the time. So that when I speak of what I believe, as a person, I cannot separate this from what I believe as an anthropologist

I believe that to understand human beings it is necessary to think of them as part of the whole living world. Our essential humanity depends not only on the complex biological structure which has been developed through the ages from very simple beginnings, but also upon the great social inventions which have been made by human beings, perpetuated by human beings, and in turn give human beings their stature as builders, thinkers, statesmen, artists, seers and prophets. I believe that each of these great inventions—language, the family, the use of tools, government, science, art and philosophy—has the quality of so combining the potentialities of every human temperament, that each can be learned and perpetuated by any group of human beings, regardless of race, and regardless of the type of civilization within which their progenitors lived, so that a newborn infant from the most primitive tribe in New Guinea is as intrinsically capable of graduation from Harvard, writing a sonnet or inventing a new form of radar as an infant born on Beacon Hill. But I believe also that once a child has been reared in New Guinea or Boston or Leningrad or Tibet, he embodies the culture within which he is reared, and differs from those who are reared elsewhere, so deeply, that only by understanding these differences can we reach an awareness which will give us a new control over our human destiny.

I believe that human nature is neither intrinsically good nor intrinsically evil, but individuals are born with different combinations of innate potentialities, and that it will depend upon how they are reared—to trust and love and experiment and create, or to fear and hate and conform—what kind of human beings they can become. I believe that we have not even begun to tap human potentialities, and that by a continuing humble but persistent study of human behavior, we can learn consciously to create civilizations within which an increasing proportion of human beings will realize more of what they have it in them to be.

I believe that human life is given meaning through the relationship which the individual's conscious goals have to the civilization, period and country within which one lives. At times the task may be to fence a wilderness, bridge a river, or rear sons to perpetuate a young colony. Today it means taking upon ourselves the task of creating one world in such a way that we both keep the future safe and leave the future free.

◆§ MARGARET MEAD, a native of Philadelphia and now a resident of New York, has roamed the world in her study of races and peoples. Her educational background includes De Pauw University, Barnard College, and Columbia University, from which she received her Doctor's degree

From 1929 to 1933 she lived in the Admiralty Islands and in New Guinea, participating in the community life and speaking the native dialects. The period 1936 to 1939 she spent in Bali

and again New Guinea Coming of Age in Samoa, An Inquiry into the Question of Cultural Stability in Polynesia, and Keep Your Powder Dry are the titles of some of her books She is that always rare person, a scientist and scholar who writes entertainingly for the layman.

Small, dark-haired Dr. Mead is now Associate Curator of Ethnology at the American Museum of Natural History in New York, and Professor of Anthropology at Columbia University.

A Touch of God's Finger

BY LAURITZ MELCHIOR

I believe that a human being can do a lot himself to shape his life. For me, the most important thing is to work hard when I work and acquire all possible knowledge in my line of work . . . and then learn how to relax in between.

My greatest relaxation is nature. I mean by that to disappear into nature—to go out in the forest with my gun, my dog, or a friend. There I will hear no telephones, receive no mail. There I can sit down and live with nature . . . feel God around me.

I feel God most when I am out in the forest and sit down on an old tree stump and see the little insects, animals and flowers around me. There I see the meaning of life and death. I see them fight each other, kill each other for existence or love and I feel the greatness of the Creator. It is the greatest way to know that there is something more than myself, over me, guiding me. It takes away one's fear for death. I know that when my time is up, I should be ready to quit—as long as I have lived happily.

And I have lived happily, because I have had a wonderful companion at my side—my wife—and we have learned to square ourselves with each other. We know that in order to have a real partnership in marriage we must each have our own individuality. If she is better able to do a certain thing, I let her take over—and she lets me do what I am better able to do. We took up our life structure hand in hand, and my darling Kleinchen has been my inspiration, my comrade, my love and my guiding angel now for over twenty-six years.

It takes many small opportunities, and friends who believe in you, as well as your own energy and will to build a career. But as an artist, my first belief must be in myself. Talent in a person is a touch of God's finger; yet any artist must work hard to grow up into his art—going slowly—acquiring all possible knowledge going with it. Only then can you stay in your art for a long period of years.

A singer must know his stage. He is, shall I say, a painter with tones for color. When I paint an operatic picture, I use a big brush with a lot of paint and a lot of colors—loud and bright—to be looked at from a distance Now concert art is another sort of painting. In every song I must create for the listener the spirit of the music and its words, and this piece of art is to be looked at from a close distance, so I have to work out the little details musically as well as in the feeling and meaning of the words.

We all know what power there is in music—it is able to pat our heads and get our tears to flow when we are in great sorrow or pain, and it is able to magnify our happiness and joy. I think a better medicine doesn't exist in the world.

◄§ LAURITZ MELCHIOR, one of the great dramatic tenors of this century, has sung the roles of Tristan, Siegfried, and Tannhäuser more often than any other artist Although now renowned as a true Wagnerian *Heldentenor*, he began his operatic career in his native Copenhagen as a baritone

A Metropolitan Opera star since 1926, he has also sung in opera houses the world over. His American and foreign honors are many and include the title of "Singer to the Royal Court at Denmark," and the French Legion of Honor.

His approach to life is as hearty and ebullient as his approach to singing. Noted for his cooking, his favorite concoctions are oxtail soup and smörgåsbord. Other interests include hunting, collecting art objects and helping the blind. Now living in a beautiful glass-walled house in the San Fernando Valley, he is a popular guest artist on radio and television, and has undertaken still another career in the movies.

An Optimist Pleads Guilty

BY JOE J. MICKLE

I MUST plead guilty to being an optimist—a long-range optimist. I like to view human progress in centuries rather than in years I do not believe progress is automatic, nor does my optimism relieve me of a sense of urgency in working for human betterment; but a long, backward glance at the human races always reassures me.

This means that I am enthusiastic about life. Henry Chester has said, "Enthusiasm is the greatest asset in the world. It is nothing more or less than faith in action."

The most difficult person for me to understand is one who is bored; yet each day I encounter those who seem dead to the glamour and challenge of life. Life has so many sides that I cannot imagine why it should ever appear tedious or uninteresting. I'd like nine lives, each in a different activity.

In Peking I once saw a sign near the railway station which read, "Your baggage forwarded in all directions " To me, life is so interesting that enthusiasm has come naturally and I've wanted to run off in a lot of directions all at once. Fortunately, my own work has been big enough to merit my full enthusiasm. This is my "faith in action."

But for me, optimism and enthusiasm can be deeply rooted and continuous only if they spring from an inner sense of the presence of God and faith in His spirit at work in the world The 139th Psalm is my inspiration, for it expresses this faith· "Oh, Lord, thou hast searched me and known me—Though I take the wings of the morning and dwell in the uttermost parts of the sea, even there shall thy hand lead me." This faith makes life more orderly and simple, yet more complete.

Thankfulness, too, is my "faith in action." I am thankful for past generations which have paid the price of human progress. I try not to take them for granted. To those who through much suffering have brought us greater freedom, broader visions and better living conditions, I feel undying gratitude. I like to turn back the hands of time to study their lives and struggles Also, I am thankful to those of my generation, particularly to those of talents different and greater than mine, who have picked up where others left off and are carrying on toward that "far-off, divine event toward which all creation moves."

But the spirit of thankfulness to my own and past generations cannot be complete without frequently lifting the face upward simply to say, "Thank You, God." In fact, with me at least, it is here that the spirit of thankfulness finds its first expression. From there I want it to flow outward toward my fellow men of whatever race, color, creed or talent.

I knew a four-year-old girl in Japan who, at the end of a wonderful day of play with her American and Japanese friends, asked permission to say her evening prayers in her own words. Then she said, "Thank You, God, for a pleasant day," hesitated a moment while she thought what should come next, then in complete sincerity added, "I hope You've had a good time too."

That prayer implies that if thankfulness is genuine it must be linked to life's actions. It is thankfulness which says to God, "I hope that this day my actions have brought You only pleasure."

◆§ JOE J. MICKLE, born and raised in Texas and educated at Southern Methodist and Columbia Universities, has been president of Centenary College of Louisiana, in Shreveport, since 1945. His primary field is history and political science, although for twenty years he taught commercial subjects at Kwansei Gakuin University in Japan.

While in Japan he closely observed the rise of militarism in that country from 1931 to 1941. This revealed to him the true nature of totalitarian governments and intensified his interest in international political organizations. In the belief that a strong federation of the leading democracies is necessary to achieve peace, he supports the work of the Atlantic Union Committee.

He has an almost equal love for the white clouds and broad vistas of the Texas plains and the rugged snow-capped mountains of Japan. Mountain climbing, baseball, chess, and photography have all contributed a share to his zest for living

The Debt of the Artist

by DIMITRI MITROPOULOS

VERY EARLY in my life, an important event took place: the discovery in my impressionable youth of the personality of St. Francis. Since that time, my main ambition has been canalized into a strong desire to serve my neighbor by putting at his disposal the fruits of my knowledge, the results of my studying and the development of my innate talent and the development of my skill as a performer, plus my love!

My dream has always been to master myself for the sake of serving better and being of more use to my fellow man.

My concern and love for him made me realize an additional responsibility which my fame as an artist brought to me, and that is my responsibility as a human being towards those of my fellow men who might look to me for guidance. Soon after I had the privilege to come to this country I realized how important it was to become an example, and I will mention two events which have reinforced this my belief.

Some years ago, during the war, I heard that the Blood Bank of the Red Cross which served in Minneapolis and its vicinity badly needed assistance Naturally, they were not able to pay for all that they needed, so I decided to take my vacation by accepting the responsible job of blood custodian. I was driving in a truck to various towns within a hundred miles of Minneapolis and taking charge of setting up the Mobile Unit in each town. The Red Cross administration thought it advisable to advertise the fact that I was working for them, in order to attract public interest. It went to the point where some people probably thought that I was going to entertain them with music during the bleeding, which I certainly would not have refused to do, in spite of the amount of work I had to do, if the doctors hadn't forbidden such an enjoyable treatment because they wouldn't be able to hear the pulses of the patients.

The next event was during the time I was conducting the Robin Hood Dell Orchestra in Philadelphia, and also during the war. There was a terrific scandal there of misguided youths in the high schools mistreating and insulting Jewish boys. Nobody seemed to be able to stop this tragic epidemic, neither the teachers in the schools nor the preachers in the churches. Finally, Mr. Samuel, at that time the mayor, had the inspired idea of bringing a popular movie star to speak to the various schools, an event which stopped, like a miracle, all those tragedies.

From that I developed the theory that all people who have the chance to enjoy the responsibility of being famous, regardless for what reason or in what profession, can be of a terrific help in this confused world of today by setting an example of sound moral thinking and integrity, as human beings as well as in their profession. I came even to the point of realizing that any skill of any kind, physical or mental, or any artistic achievement, unless it is based on a moral purpose, cannot claim to have any value or any plausible reason to exist.

DIMITRI MITROPOULOS came to his post of Musical Director of the Philharmonic-Symphony Orchestra of New York after a spectacular conducting career in his native Athens and in the music capitals of Europe.

Mr Mitropoulos maintains bachelor quarters near Carnegie Hall. Rising at dawn, he studies scores until it's time to walk over to the Hall for rehearsals Incidentally, if ever there was a "dedicated" musician, he is that man He knows by heart not only hundreds of scores, but also every bar's rehearsal number. Lunchtime finds him, he says, as hungry as a blacksmith. Following this repast, an Hellenic nap enables him to accomplish two days' work in one

Sharply chiseled features and a lithe figure make him seem tall Nowadays, a thin wreath of hair half encircles a finely molded skull. He is an honorary doctor of music several times over, and wears the ribbon of an Officer of the Legion of Honor.

The Hidden Vitality of Human Beings

BY NEWBOLD MORRIS

WHAT HAS BEEN the most appealing part of the development of the "American Dream"? To some of us, perhaps, the most dramatic phase of our development has been the ceaseless energy of the pioneers, the era of empire building, and finally the apotheosis of free enterprise—our industrial development. Others are thrilled by the capacity of the American people, normally peace-loving and slow to anger, to organize in an all-out effort to resist threats to their freedom.

Yes, all of these things stir the imagination. But to me they are the outward and visible sign of an inward and spiritual vitality. Some of us came to this continent three centuries ago and take great pride in tradition. Others may have landed at the international airport at Idlewild yesterday. But nearly all of us came as fugitives from the tyrannies and hatreds of the Old World.

I believe America has vitality because of a restless force we call "human endeavor." It is this endeavor which has resulted in the lifting of averages and the spreading of opportunities It is based on the conviction that once an individual has a fair start he or she can rise to great heights, regardless of circumstances of birth or racial origin. This is my conviction and it is, in other words, a belief in the human spirit.

It is for those who are strong to help the weak; for those who are sound in mind and body to help those afflicted; for those who live in the sunlight to dispel shadows wherever they lengthen To me, this is what life is all about. It is why I believe that when we decided upon a system of government-subsidized education, we passed an important milestone in our history, and that when we adopted public health programs to fight the ravages of disease, to reduce infant mortality, and even to afford prenatal care for expectant mothers, we were continuing along the road toward the goals in which I believe.

I feel that we took another step toward a better world when we adopted workmen's compensation laws, unemployment insurance, social security, and aid to dependent children. And I believe that we were doing even more to realize these goals when, awakening to the social evils of cheerless, unsanitary, unsafe tenements, we decided to tax ourselves in order to subsidize low-rent public housing for persons of low income. I could not be true to my beliefs about my duty toward my fellow men if I did not work for these things.

Some call our civilization a Christian civilization; others call it democracy. When it succeeds it is a little bit of both, and when it works we need not have fear of threats to our freedom.

❧ NEWBOLD MORRIS, a lawyer who believes passionately in good government, is one of the most energetic political reformers New York City has ever had. As president of the City Council and, occasionally, Acting Mayor under Mayor F. H. La Guardia, he waged an effective battle against corruption and waste.

Mr. Morris comes of a long and distinguished line of public men. He is the descendant of three mayors of New York City, a Governor of New Jersey, and innumerable Congressmen and judges. Gouverneur Morris and Lewis Morris of Revolutionary fame were also his ancestors He is a son-in-law of the great American jurist, Judge Learned Hand His school was Groton and his college Yale. He is six feet three

Mr Morris has championed such cultural and theatrical projects as New York's well-known City Center. The story is told of how he took up figure skating merely for exercise and became so proficient that he won the Middle Atlantic Championship.

The Greeks Had an Answer

BY PROF. GILBERT MURRAY

IN TRYING TO SAY what I really believe I cannot recite one of the traditional creeds, Christian, Jewish, Moslem, Buddhist, or the like. Most of us are born into one of them, and which it is depends simply on what country and what parents we come from. A great mystery surrounds us, in which the human mind can at best catch glimpses and express itself in metaphors

For myself, I come on my mother's side from a family of teachers, almost of schoolma'ams, and grew up occasionally—accordingly— a good, obedient little boy who kept all the rules. On my father's side, however, I came of a line of Irish rebels, always suspicious of authorities and deeply prejudiced in favor of the underdog. I loved new ideas and poetry; so naturally in my teens I fell deeply under the influence of Shelley "Prometheus Unbound" was for some years to me almost a sacred book. Such poetry and such a religion, proclaiming a rejection of all the oppressors who misrule the world, all the superstitions that cripple man's mind and prevent his going straight as the crow flies towards perfection! An illusion, of course. Perhaps I was slow in growing out of it.

The other main influence that has gone to forming my beliefs has been that of ancient Greece. I could hardly have escaped it, having been a Professor of Greek most of my life, from twenty-three to seventy. It got hold of me first, I suppose, by the charm of its poetry. Then, it seemed to me that the great Greek thinkers were mostly facing the same problems as ourselves, but facing them more freely and frankly, not hampered by all the complexities and inherited conventions that confuse us today. They did sincerely try to understand Truth and Justice and the Good Life.

Then, at last, in 1914 came the shock of the Great War, bringing for me, as for so many people, not any change of belief but a great change of focus. The prevention of war became the thing that mattered most in the world. I took part in the founding of the League of Nations, and for thirty years now I have been working in that cause, learning, I think, a good deal by the way. It needed more than enthusiasm. It needed patience and experience and common sense It needed day by day far more knowledge than I possessed But I found good guides and companions. I learned to think less of abstract principles and less still of party catchwords and slogans I have found among all parties, and all religions, men inspired by the great movement that leads towards peace, outward and inward. I feel much truth in an old Greek philosopher's saying, "The helping of man by man is God."

◄§ GILBERT MURRAY is world famous as a Greek scholar, poet and dramatist. As a boy, he left his native Australia for England After attending Merchant Taylors' School, he studied at St. John's College, Oxford. In 1888, when only twenty-two, he was elected Fellow of New College Beginning then, as Arnold Bennett said, "he shed his light-giving brilliance over the world." From 1908 to 1936 he was Regius Professor of Greek at Oxford and in 1926 lectured at Harvard as Charles Eliot Norton Professor of Poetry.

President of the International Committee of Intellectual Co-operation from 1928 to 1940, he now serves as joint-president of the United Nations Association of Great Britain. Even after a serious illness in 1946 he continued to work at his scholarly pursuits at his home in Boar's Hill, Oxford. His noble verse translations of the Greek dramatists represent a permanent contribution to English literature.

How to Refill an Empty Life

BY ALBERT J. NESBITT

ONE DAY about fifteen years ago I suddenly came face to face with myself and realized there was something quite empty about my life. My friends and associates perhaps didn't see it. By the generally accepted standards, I was "successful," I was head of a prosperous manufacturing concern and I led what is usually referred to as an "active" life, both socially and in business. But it didn't seem to me to be adding up to anything. I was going around in circles. I worked hard, played hard, and pretty soon I discovered I was hitting the highballs harder than I needed. I wasn't a candidate for Alcoholics Anonymous, but to be honest with myself I had to admit I was drinking more than was good for me. It may have been out of sheer boredom.

I began to wonder what to do. It occurred to me that I might have gotten myself too tightly wrapped up in my job, to the sacrifice of the basic but nonmaterialistic values of life. It struck me abruptly that I was being quite selfish, that my major interest in people was in what they meant to me, what they represented as business contacts or employees, not what I might mean to them. I remembered that as my mother sent me to Sunday school as a boy, and encouraged me to sing in the church choir, she used to tell me that the value of what she called a good Christian background was in having something to tie to. I put in a little thought recalling the Golden Rule and some of the other first principles of Christianity. I began to get interested in YMCA work.

It happened that just at this time we were having some bitter fights with the union at our plant. Then one day it occurred to me: What really is their point of view, and why? I began to see a basis for their suspicions, their often chip-on-shoulder point of view, and I determined to do something about it.

We endeavored to apply—literally apply—Christian principles to

127

our dealings with employees, to practice, for example, something of the Golden Rule. The men's response, once they were convinced we were sincere, was remarkable. The effort has paid for its pains, and I don't mean in dollars. I mean in dividends of human dignity, of a man's pride in his job and in the company, knowing that he is no longer just a cog but a live personal part of it and that it doesn't matter whether he belongs to a certain church or whether the pigmentation of his skin is light or dark.

But I can speak with most authority on how this change of attitude affected me and my personal outlook on life. Perhaps, again, many of my friends did not notice the difference.

But I noticed it. That feeling of emptiness, into which I was pouring cocktails out of boredom, was filling up instead with a purpose: to live a full life with an awareness and an appreciation of other people. I do not pretend for a second that I have suddenly become a paragon. My faults are still legion and I know them.

But it seems to me better to have a little religion and practice it than think piously and do nothing about it. I feel better adjusted, more mature than I ever have in my life before I have no fear. I say this not boastfully but in all humility. The actual application of Christian principles has changed my life.

ALBERT J. NESBITT is a Philadelphia industrialist—the president of John J. Nesbitt, Inc. His home is in suburban Ambler, and like many another country squire, he enjoys donning a pink coat and riding to hounds. During the Second World War, he served as adviser to the War Production Board.

Mr. Nesbitt devotes much of his spare time to raising funds for charitable causes. At present he is President of the Young Men's Christian Association of Philadelphia and vicinity and is also President of the United Fund Another presidency he holds is that of the Philadelphia Council of Churches.

A member of the Board of Trustees of the Pennsylvania State College, he holds honorary degrees from both Drexel Institute of Technology and Ursinus College. He is at once a hard-headed businessman and a warm-hearted human, who believes strongly in the continuing power of the Golden Rule.

The Law of Shared Investment

BY BONARO W. OVERSTREET

IT SURPRISES ME to find out in how many areas of life I have doubts and unanswered questions rather than beliefs. It surprises me even more to find that, in many of these areas, a change from doubts and questions to beliefs would feel to me like a change for the worse, not for the better.

Perhaps I'm saying that I have come up to one of my beliefs on the bias, have stumbled over it before I knew it was there: the belief, namely, that human nature is the sort of thing that does well to keep a considerable number of doubt-areas as areas to grow in. I didn't always feel this way. As an adolescent I had beliefs galore, and relatively few doubts. Now I have doubts galore and only a few hard-working beliefs. Most of them, as a matter of fact, reduce to one, variously applied. I believe that for creatures like ourselves, in a system like ours, the law of shared involvement and reciprocity in good will is the only sound law by which to live. I mean live and let live, yes, but something more.

Being physically in, and emotionally of, this psychological age, this twentieth century, I think and speak most comfortably in the language of my time. I rest my hypotheses most easily upon the knowledge of my time with such of the past as has been drawn up into that knowledge. So I find it more natural to talk of emotional health and ill-health than of good and evil in man. I find that my concerns cluster more spontaneously around problems of human fulfillment than of human salvation.

I believe that such portion of the psychic universe as is housed in me—that is, my person, myself—will be frustrated and distorted in its growth to the extent that I frustrate and distort other lives. I believe that to do to others as I would have them do to me is not simply a law of duty, it is also a law of health, that we violate at our own risk. Where we violate it, we injure ourselves; inhibit our powers;

blunt our sense of reality; condemn ourselves to fear, guilt, and hostility, and progressively isolate ourselves from our human kind, so that we feel alone and under threat.

I believe that the line of psychic demarcation between one person and another is less clearly and rigidly drawn than we think. The separateness of our physical bodies has deceived us. It has given us the notion that we are separate as psychological entities, and that our full psychological stature can, so to speak, be achieved through self-contained processes. I am sure this is not true. I am sure that the "I" that I now am is most significantly a product of all that has gone on between me and other human beings through all the years of my living Where my relationships to others are soundly growing, I am growing. Where they are halted in their growth, I am halted Where they are twisted in their growth, I am twisted in mine.

This belief about human involvements leads to another: that self-respect and respect for others go together. I do not believe it is possible, except superficially, to think well of ourselves and ill of our human fellows, or to think well of them and ill of ourselves Our attitude toward ourselves and toward others is one: it is our attitude toward human nature

As an extension of this, I believe the best situations for us to live and grow in are those geared to equality equality of respect; equality of rights I do not believe we can attain our psychological stature, our real human stature, either by leaning on others or by trying to outdo others and gain power over them I am for the level look of equality and the cordial look of friendliness between man and man.

◄§ BONARO W. OVERSTREET is a poet and teacher who is fond of cooking, gardening and playing the mandolin Half of the year she and her husband live on the Overstreet farm in Vermont, the other half in Mill Valley, California.

After an education at the University of California and Columbia, she taught at California until she "graduated into marriage and a full writing career." Her first book was The Poetic Way of Release, followed later by two books of poems, Footsteps on the Earth and American Reasons. Her deep interest in people turned her toward the richly developing fields of psychology and psychotherapy, and she has written a number of books on personality The most recent is Understanding Fear in Ourselves and Others.

As poet and psychologist, she brings a warm imagination and a disciplined mind to the service of humanity.

The Hidden World Around Us

BY PROF. HARRY A. OVERSTREET

EVER SINCE Socrates was introduced to my adolescent mind, he has been one chief master of my thinking. What he believed still seems to me to be indispensable for carrying on an intelligent and responsible life. He believed *that he did not know* For myself, I have come to change his negative into a positive I know that there is far more in this universe for me to know than I now know.

I recently had a dramatic illustration of this. My wife and I, driving through Arizona, stopped at a "collector's shop" in Tucson, where stones and minerals of many kinds were on display. In the course of the visit, we were taken into a small room where rocks were laid out on shelves. They were quite ordinary-looking rocks. Had I seen them on some hillside, I would not have given them a second thought. Then the man closed the door so that the room was in total darkness and turned on an ultraviolet lamp.

Instantly the prosaic rocks leaped into a kind of glory. Brilliant colors of an indescribable beauty were there before our eyes.

A very simple thing—and yet a very tremendous thing—had happened. A certain power had been snapped on; and a hidden world leaped into life.

As I look at my universe and walk among my fellow humans, I have the deep belief that hidden realities are all around us. These hidden realities are there in the physical world; and they are there, also, in the human world. If I am foolish enough to think that I see all there is to be seen in front of my eyes, I simply miss the glory.

I believe, then, that my chief job in life—and my astonishing privilege—is to snap on an extra power so that I can see what my naked eyes—or my naked mind—cannot now see. I believe that I have to do this particularly with my human fellows. My ordinary eyes tend to stop short at those opaque envelopes we call human bodies. But we have learned that by turning on a certain power we can penetrate to the inside of these envelopes.

We call this extra power "imagination." At its highest, we call it "empathy," the power to see through and to feel through to the inner life of other human beings. It is a kind of ultraviolet lamp of our psychic life. When we turn on this lamp of imaginative sensitivity, we make the prosaic human beings around us come excitingly alive.

Zona Gale once set down as the first article of her creed: "I believe in expanding the areas of my awareness." I'd do the same. If I expand the areas of my awareness, I move understandingly into realities beyond me. When I move into them understandingly, I know what I can do and what I should do. If I don't move in understandingly, if I stay in ignorance on the outside, then, in all likelihood, I will do mistaken things.

The great principle of love depends upon this. He who loves another tries truly to understand the other. We can reverse this· he who tries truly to understand another is not likely to hate that other.

Socrates gave no finished catalogue of the "truths" of the world. He gave, rather, the impulse to search. This is far better, I feel, than dogmatic certainty. When we are aware that there are glories of life still hidden from us, we walk humbly before the Great Unknown But we do more than this. we try manfully to increase our powers of seeing and feeling so that we can turn what is still unknown into what is warmly and understandingly known. . . . This, I believe, is our great human adventure.

HARRY A. OVERSTREET spent his undergraduate days at the University of California before moving on to do graduate work at Oxford. Upon his return, he taught philosophy at his alma mater and later headed the philosophy department at the College of the City of New York. Retiring some years before the normal time, he decided to use the United States as his classroom.

Lecturing to adults and discussing ideas with them has been one of his richest experiences. In recent years, he has appeared jointly with his wife, Bonaro, sharing with her equally both platform and ideas Out of these shared experiences they have individually written their many books on the growth possibilities of the human personality. Mr. Overstreet's best-known works are *Influencing Human Behavior, The Mature Mind*, and the recently published *The Great Enterprise*.

His philosophy is summed up in his favorite Aristotelian dictum. "Man is what he has it in him to become"

A Shining Day Will Come

by SAUL K. PADOVER

A CANDID STATEMENT of faith becomes, for me, a concentrated spiritual autobiography. My fundamental beliefs are the products of three converging influences that have been silently at work within my personality. history, America, and Jefferson.

As a student of history I have been impressed again and again by man's potentialities for good and evil. I spent my childhood in Vienna. The atmosphere of the dying Austrian Empire made me sensitive to comparative politics and history. Gradually the conviction grew in me that man everywhere, regardless of race or region or climate, is his own worst enemy or best friend By and large, human beings themselves create their own heavens or hells. They do so because, of all the creatures on earth, they alone have the intelligence and imagination to change their environment.

My first American home was Detroit. This great Midwestern metropolis, the very essence of twentieth-century American industrialism, stimulated my imagination. From the inspiring history of America I have learned what good will, intelligence, and creative application can accomplish. It is one of my beliefs that the opportunities of social and human well-being in America are still inexhaustible.

And this brings me to Thomas Jefferson. His influence on my spiritual and intellectual life has been continuous and pervasive. I think I know by now every word he has ever written; I feel inside of me the very rhythm of his thought. His life and personality have been to me sources of spiritual strength and inspiration. Jefferson never failed me in any crisis.

What I have learned from him, in brief, has been an abiding faith in human potentialities. I would call this the religion of democratic humanism. Following Jefferson's optimistic faith—despite examples of horror and bloodshed in recent times—I believe that man can and

133

should be kind and just to his fellows; that man can and should strive for constant spiritual and social improvement . . . and keep the avenues of opportunity always open for himself and his fellow men. To state it negatively, I believe with all my heart that cruelty, injustice, and intolerance are social crimes that should be punished as severely as physical ones

It is a cardinal article of faith with me that there is no limit to what men in society can achieve. In this context, I believe that the good, just and happy life cannot be achieved in any society where power, political or economic, is monopolized in the hands of a single person or single group I hold, with Jefferson, that only inside a democratic society, even if it is imperfect, can human beings make a successful effort to attain happiness

And finally, I believe that all these human goals are attainable by men of all races and creeds, and that, if we use our social intelligence and the ample tools of science, a day will come when there is no bloodshed, hatred, and disease, and no slums and no poverty, and no destructive fears of the unknown.

◄§ SAUL K PADOVER, who holds degrees from Wayne and Chicago Universities, is dean of the School of Politics at the New School for Social Research in New York He was born in Austria of American parents and spent his early years abroad Previously a historian, government official, and foreign correspondent, he is still active in many diverse fields Besides his deanship, he writes extensively within his two major fields. American politics and European institutions.

During the last war he was an O S.S. intelligence officer, spending nearly a year at the front, and was awarded "for distinguished service" the Bronze Star, a Presidential citation, and the ribbon of the French Legion of Honor.

He spends his summers in Europe, lecturing to young people, and studying cathedrals—a favorite relaxation One of his monumental works is the biography Jefferson His work reflects an attempt to base a modern political sociology upon Jefferson's ideals

Growing in the Middle Ground

BY ANNE PHIPPS

I BELIEVE that my beliefs are changing Nothing is positive. Perhaps I am in a stage of metamorphosis which will one day have me emerging complete, sure of everything. Perhaps I shall spend my life searching.

Until this winter, I believed in outward things, in beauty as I found it in nature and art. Beauty passed, swift and sure, from the outside to the inside, bringing intense emotion. I felt a formless faith when I rode through summer woods, when I heard the counterpoint of breaking waves, when I held a flower in my hand. There was the same inspiration from art—here and there, in flashes—in seeing for the first time the delicacy of a white jade vase, or the rich beauty of a rug, in hearing a passage of music played almost perfectly, in watching Markova dance Giselle, most of all in reading. Other people's consciousness, their sensitivity to emotion, color, sound, their feeling for form, instructed me. The necessity for beauty I found to be the highest good, the human soul's greatest gift. *It was not, I felt, all.*

This winter I came to college. The questions put to me changed. Lists of facts and "who dragged whom how many times around the walls of what?" lost importance. Instead I was asked eternal questions: What is Beauty? What is Truth? What is God? I talked about faith with other students. I read St. Augustine and Tolstoy. I wondered if I hadn't been worshiping around the edges. Nature and art were the edges, an inner faith was the center. I discovered, really discovered, that I had a soul. Just sitting in the sun one day, I realized the shattering meaning of St. Augustine's statement that the sun and the moon, all the wonders of nature, are not God's "first works," but second to the spiritual works.

I had, up till then, perceived spiritual beauty only through the outward; it had come into me. Now, I am groping towards an inner spiritual consciousness that will be able to go out from me. I am lost in the middle ground; I am learning.

ANNE PHIPPS, daughter of a New York banker, is a bright-eyed, attractive undergraduate at Bryn Mawr College. She was born in New York in 1932 and is a graduate of the Chapin School She majors in French at Bryn Mawr and is spending her junior year at the Sorbonne in Paris

Her contribution, above, presents a charming "picture" of a sensitive American girl growing up—and growing, as well, into an awareness of the world and its problems and rewards.

Her interest in the world about her, indeed, has prompted her to spend her vacations in traveling. She has toured the United States, has journeyed to Mexico and Canada, and through Europe.

Away from her studies, Miss Phipps likes to devote time to her hobbies, which are riding and deep-sea fishing. After graduation, as an "emerging world citizen," she says she hopes to work in the field of international relations.

I Call Things As I See Them

BY RALPH PINELLI

AN UMPIRE has to make instant decisions. I've learned to call things as I see them This helps me make a quick reply to such an important and personal question as my belief. My philosophy of life is simple, with a vital driving force.

I believe in my God, my family, my country and baseball.

Including baseball may seem out of place in this statement, but I firmly believe that baseball, more than being just a national pastime, is beneficially bound up with American life—certainly with my own. It helped develop me physically as a boy It taught me teamwork and ability to co-operate with others Another thing, it taught me to try to play according to the rules of the game This has helped me throughout life.

My parents came to this country from Italy as poor immigrants. I grew up at a time when even a high-school education was out of reach. My formal education never went beyond the elementary grades But the lessons I learned at home, at church and on the playground have carried me through.

I believe firmly in higher education. My son was assigned to a baseball contract when he was still in high school but I insisted on a clause permitting him a full four-year college course before starting professional ball.

I believe that even more important than a college education, though, is the good solid practical and religious training in the home and at church My mother taught me a proper scale of values and trained me to live up to them. I still remember the sand-lot game I had to leave before the final inning so I could get on my Sunday suit and be at church in time for Confirmation.

Experience has proved my belief in the importance of the family. This is where good, useful citizens come from. My wife and I have enjoyed the companionship of some thirty-five years of married life,

137

and we have had the happiness of seeing our two sons grow into manhood and start their own families We never had the pleasure of having a daughter, but now we happily share three granddaughters and five grandsons Our happiness with them is a great consolation and comfort against the older years when many a couple grow lonely

I have found strength and consolation in my church, and I have found peace and help in humble daily prayer when I praise God for His goodness and ask Him to "forgive me my trespasses as I forgive others," and beg His blessings for myself and my family and friends.

So these are the things I believe in·

My God, who has given me a personal destiny and who deserves all praise and service;

My family, who have given me happiness and strength;

My country, which has given me every opportunity to live my life according to my conscience;

And baseball, which has given me healthy recreation and solid training for life.

This is my theology and philosophy of life.

◅§ RALPH "BABE" PINELLI is completing his eighteenth year as an umpire for the National League. A man of medium build, his smiling brown eyes belie the firmness with which he controls a baseball game Prior to his umpiring days, he was an active player for eight years in the National and American Leagues and eight in the Pacific Coast League

"Babe's" formal education under the Christian Brothers was interrupted in the fourth grade when his father, an Italian immigrant, was killed in the San Francisco earthquake of 1906. Second oldest of four children, he had to help support his family, which he did by selling newspapers and working in an iron foundry.

He is married, has two sons, both graduates of Notre Dame, one of whom is a physician, the other a businessman During baseball's off-season, "Babe" lives in San Francisco, where he spends some time getting better acquainted with his eight grandchildren.

Destination Through Darkness

BY BENTZ PLAGEMANN

ON A CERTAIN MIDNIGHT in August during the last war I found myself on a stretcher in the bottom of a small boat, lost in the Bay of Naples. A few days before that I had contracted poliomyelitis at sea, and when my legs became paralyzed the captain felt it was imperative to get me ashore no matter what the hazards. The harbor was completely blacked out, lighted only by the glow of Mount Vesuvius; our ship had never been there before, and the boys operating the small boat became lost. Overhead there were enemy planes, but at last, by the illumination of bursting shells from the shore batteries, the boys saw the dock and took me ashore.

Sometimes since that night I have imagined that this dramatic incident contained within itself my whole attitude toward life, for very often it seems to me that I am helpless, adrift in darkness, beset by dangers, proceeding to a strange and hidden destination. Yet I survived that experience and walk again, just as I have survived other personal problems, because of a hard-won conviction that if I keep faith with myself, if I am patient and do not despair, sooner or later, possibly during the darkest moment, the revelation will not be wanting to light my way a few steps onward to whatever destination I am approaching.

As a child I was taught by my religious instructors that I would never be tempted to evil beyond my power to resist. In later years I have translated this axiom into other terms. Now I say that in the same way, I think that life cannot pose problems to me which I cannot surmount. There is nothing of cant or textbook morality in this belief of mine. I have no knowledge of formal philosophy and doubtless I have arrived at very elementary conclusions known to many men, but it seems to me that I could not have been created in any other way. I have a simple belief in a personal God, also given to me as a child, and in some area of instinctive reasoning I believe

139

that when this God created me He presented me with an equation which I must work out in terms of the living of my life. It is a difficult equation, I know that, but it was constructed to fit my possibilities, and while it will take my whole life to see it through, I believe that its successful conclusion is within my power. To reach this balance of my forces is, I believe, the whole purpose of my existence.

To be patient with my own failures, not to fall into despair—this is my greatest problem. Within my human limitations I am aware of only the barest outline of my possibilities, and every day I fail in some way. Yet I remind myself, when I do not keep faith with myself, when I fall into my weaknesses, that the important fact is that I know when I have failed, and consequently every day I arrive more nearly to a knowledge of myself. I find consolation in thinking of my failures as guideposts to a better realization of myself.

I suppose I could sum it all up by saying that I believe in myself. Or in whatever it is in myself which makes it possible for me to dream of a better person than I am now, and which gives me deep pleasure in the act of working, however painfully, toward a happier fulfillment of my being.

BENTZ PLAGEMANN, who has written several novels and many short stories, had no formal education beyond high school Instead of going to college he worked in a bookstore, borrowing a book nightly to take home and read.

Despite this bookish background, he believes that it was in the Navy, during World War II. that his real education began. As a Pharmacist's Mate, he served in the Norfolk Naval Hospital, when casualties from North Africa overflowed onto cots in the corridors. Later, while on a landing ship in the Mediterranean, he was stricken with polio.

From observation of his own suffering and that of others, he says he came to realize for the first time the validity and the power of the New Testament message of spiritual rebirth. He tries to convey in his writing something of this hard-won, but invaluable, lesson.

A Man's Will to His Son

BY DICK POWELL

As I WATCH my young son crawling on the floor, trying to learn to
walk, I am filled with a desire to help him. Not with just a steadying
hand. I want to pass on to him as he grows up some practical, work-
able philosophy of life that will make his steps sure and strong in the
face of the next fifty years. I'd like to give him something new, something startling, something even atomic in its originality But I don't
know any new sure-fire philosophies with a lifetime guarantee.

I can and will pass on to him those things I've believed in during
my attempt to live a full and useful life. Even they are not original;
others passed them on to me. I won't mind repeating—and I hope he
won't mind hearing—over and over again all the quotations, rules,
proverbs, even bromides that I live with "Honesty is the best policy"
—"A stitch in time saves nine"—"A rolling stone gathers no moss"—
"Laugh and the world laughs with you, weep and you weep alone."
And including by all means "Do unto others as you would have them
do unto you," and many others.

I'll try to make them sound as little like slogans as possible. This
won't be easy. They have been repeated so often in such a ponderous
and sanctimonious manner that their sharp true meaning seems to
have been dulled. But I'll tell him these things because I believe in
them. I believe in them because they are truth and are the results of
the thinking and living of thousands of God-fearing people before
me Some of these thoughts were even from people who had no organized religion but realized the necessity of them if they were to live
successfully in a group.

As a boy, I sang in the Catholic children's choir. After my voice
changed into what the neighbors called the loudest tenor in the city,
I sang in every choir in town—Baptist, Episcopalian, Presbyterian,
Jewish synagogue, the Masonic Hall and many, many others. I belonged to the First Christian Church but I never sang there because

141

I was too busy elsewhere. I like to think that I had a liberal religious education even if it was from the choir lofts.

I learned to believe that not all men are good, but that most men want to be good I believe in God, and whether I try to have Him hear me through the temples, the churches or even from the sidewalks of the street, it is to the same end. I want always to try to be vigilant, to help see to it that man shall forever have the right to worship God and call to Him whenever and wherever he pleases, within the bounds of the society he lives in.

My son will soon walk. He will start living in society the minute he starts playing with the boy next door. I know that these things I believe will help him live better with the boy next door, the thousands in the state, the millions in the country, and, yes, even the billions in this great world.

§ DICK POWELL is a self-made, able, thoughtful man, successful not only in his career but in his life

He started with the Bell Telephone Company in his home town of Little Rock, Arkansas. There the girls, and folk generally, liked his singing and liked him. He went on to Hollywood to become "America's Boy Friend—the nice guy down the street" He starred in Warner Brothers' first musicals, *Flirtation Walk, Anchors Aweigh,* and many others. Then came a "new" Dick Powell. He became a tough man in detective films, and his radio programs changed from the type of his famous *Hollywood Hotel* to *Richard Diamond, Private Detective*

Handsome, six feet tall, Dick remains a top star, while starting also to produce pictures and television shows His hobbies have been sailing and flying He and his wife, June Allyson, share many interests, of which by far the chief one is the raising of their children.

The Wisdom of a King

BY J. ARTHUR RANK

I AM NOT one of those people who believe that the world is "going to the dogs" or that there is no hope for civilization. I have a great faith in human nature and I believe civilization can be salvaged from the total wreck it has almost become, but I am quite sure that salvation can come not through political or economic factors but through divine intervention.

I believe that most of the ills of the world—and the world is only a mixed collection of individuals like you and me—are not traceable to physical or mental causes but result from a lack of spiritual power in you and me caused by the low priority we give to the development of the spiritual side of our being and to the lack of faith that God will give us His Holy Spirit if we ask Him.

What do I believe? Is my belief of any value in an age when the main topics of conversation are based on atomic warfare and distrust? This I believe—that God is our Father and loves us and that Christ died for the world and came to show the world what God was like and to teach the world the way to have a joyous life and be free from fear—and the world includes you and me.

I believe, too, that only by following the commandments He has given us can we be delivered from the spirit of defeatism which haunts so many people today.

I believe in the fellowship of the Holy Spirit. I believe that without the influence of the Holy Spirit in our lives it is impossible for us to do our daily job effectively, whether that job be the ordinary everyday task of bringing up children in the home or whether it be the high and great responsibility to which our young and gracious Queen has been called

I believe in faith in humanity and a faith in a God who understands and guides me, and against which the fears, trials and disappointments of our day cannot prevail.

If I were asked to express this faith in words I could find no better way than did our late King during his Christmas broadcast in the fateful days of 1939:

"I said to the Man who stood at the Gate of the Year, 'Give me a light that I may tread safely into the unknown.' And he replied, 'Go out into the darkness and put your hand into the hand of God. That shall be to you better than light and safer than a known way.' "

This I believe with all my heart.

J. ARTHUR RANK makes flour for England's bread and motion pictures for the world's theaters. He ended his formal education at seventeen to take a thirteen-hour-a-day, ten-shillings-a-week job in his father's flour mills He eventually became highly successful in this business, but it is in his second calling, the movies, that he has achieved world fame

His interest in motion pictures began with religious films. While his secular film interests are now far-reaching (he produced *Henry V* and *Hamlet*), he has never forgotten his original reason for entering the field—a belief that pictures should serve as well as entertain.

Married to the daughter of a former Lord Mayor of London, he has two daughters. Most of his leisure is spent at his country home near Reigate where he golfs, shoots, and breeds dogs. The local Sunday school class which he teaches gives him his deepest satisfaction, he says.

One Girl Changed My Life

BY ROSE RESNICK

MY CHILDHOOD and adolescence were a joyous outpouring of energy, a ceaseless quest for expression, skill and experience. School was only a background to the supreme delight of lessons in music, dance and dramatics, and the thrill of sojourns in the country, theaters, concerts and books—big Braille books that came with me on streetcars, to the table and to bed. Then, one night at a high-school dance, a remark not intended for my ears stabbed my youthful bliss. "That girl— what a pity she is blind." Blind! That ugly word that implied everything dark, blank, rigid and helpless. Quickly, I turned and called out, "Please don't feel sorry for me—I'm having lots of fun." But the fun was not to last

With the advent of college, I was brought to grips with the problem of earning a living. Part-time teaching of piano and harmony, and, upon graduation, occasional concerts and lectures, proved only partial sources of livelihood In terms of time and effort involved, the financial remuneration was disheartening. This induced within me searing self-doubt and dark moods of despondency. Adding to my dismal sense of inadequacy was the repeated experience of seeing my sisters and friends go off to exciting dates. How grateful I was for my piano, where, through Chopin, Beethoven and Brahms, I could mingle my longing and seething energy with theirs, and where I could dissolve my frustration in the beauty and grandeur of their conceptions.

Then, one day I met a girl, a wonderful girl, an Army nurse, whose faith and stability were to change my whole life As our acquaintance ripened into friendship, she discerned, behind a shell of gaiety, my recurring plateaus of depression She said, "Stop knocking on closed doors. Keep up your beautiful music—I know your opportunity will come. You're trying too hard Why don't you relax, and have you ever tried praying?" The idea was strange to me It sounded too simple. Somehow, I had always operated on the premise that, if you wanted something in this world, you had to go out and get it for yourself. Yet sincerity and hard work had yielded only meager returns, and I was willing to try anything.

Experimentally, self-consciously, I cultivated a daily practice of prayer I said, "God, show me the purpose for which You sent me to this world. Help me to be of use to myself and to humanity."

In the years to follow, the answers began to arrive, clear and satisfying beyond my most optimistic anticipation One of the answers is Enchanted Hills, where, each year, my nurse friend and I have the privilege of seeing blind children come alive in God's out-of-doors. Others are the never-ending sources of pleasure and comfort I have found in friendship, in great music and, most important of all, in my growing belief that as I attune my life to divine revelation, I draw closer to God and, through Him, to immortality.

ᴥᔧᔦᐁ Rose RESNICK put aside a lifelong ambition to be a concert pianist in order to become executive director of Recreation for the Blind, Inc, of San Francisco Born in New York City, she was one of a family of ten. Aided by "The Lighthouse," she was taught how to enjoy and work in a world which she could not see. A series of earned scholarships enabled her to graduate from Hunter College in 1934. Later, she received a Master's degree from the University of California.

Now primarily concerned with helping children, Miss Resnick devotes much of her time to out-of-door camps and other activities which Recreation for the Blind sponsors. Her favorite pastimes are ice-skating and dancing. She believes that the real keys to happiness lie in health, education, a variety of skills and interests, a positive outlook on life, and an eagerness to serve mankind. These, she feels, can add luster and a deeper meaning to any life.

If I Were a Dictator

BY QUENTIN REYNOLDS

IF I WERE A DICTATOR the first book I would burn would be the Bible.
I'd burn it because I'd realize that the whole concept of democracy
came out of that book. "Democracy" is a Greek word which means
rule by the people, but even at the height of its ancient glory Athens
was not a democracy. The Greeks gave us the word for it but the
Bible gave us the philosophy and the way which we call democracy.

Remember the story of young David the shepherd boy as told in
the Book of Samuel. David came to the sorely pressed army of Israel
bringing supplies to his brothers. Now for forty days the arrogant
Goliath, champion of the Philistines' army, had challenged any single man of Israel to combat but none had been able to prevail against
him Young David asked permission of King Saul to try his luck.
There was no other volunteer so Saul accepted his services And Saul
fitted David out in his own armor, his own coat of mail and helmet of
brass, and gave him a huge sword But this heavy array of armor and
weapons didn't fit the shepherd boy and he had the good sense to
know it. He dropped the sword and slipped out of the heavy armor.
The one weapon he knew how to use was the slingshot. So, choosing
five smooth stones from a brook, he advanced upon Goliath and slew
him David in Saul's armor meant defeat; David fighting his own
way and with weapons he knew meant victory. Young David was an
individualist, in a real sense a nonconformer, for he refused to use
the traditional weapons. And wise King Saul did not confuse conformity and loyalty

Nor did the Savior. When Jesus chose twelve men to be with
Him and carry on His mission after He was gone He didn't select
a group of rubber stamps. There was Peter, the impetuous; Andrew,
the plodder; John, the poet; Simon, the fiery zealot; Thomas, the
melancholy. They were not stereotyped "yes" men. He put a pre-
mium on their infinite variety. They were united by their very dif-

147

ferences. He encouraged them to question His most fundamental beliefs and in open discussion their doubts were resolved and their faith strengthened.

You don't have to read political science or study constitutional law to understand democracy or to realize that, when individuality is suppressed, society suffers; when originality is thwarted, progress is halted. You only have to read the Bible to provide understanding. Let Saul have his heavy armor if he wishes and let David have his slingshot and his five smooth stones Let each of us be as impetuous as Peter or as slow and plodding as Andrew From the point of view of a dictator who can rule only as long as individual thoughts and ideas and conduct are suppressed, these are dangerous thoughts to be lurking in the mind of man. Yes, if I were a dictator the first book I would burn would be the Bible.

◄§ QUENTIN REYNOLDS, who entered journalism as a sports writer for the New York World, is now editor of the United Nations World Upon his graduation from Brown University, he enrolled in law school at night while he worked during the day. By the time he had earned his degree, he was an experienced reporter.

As a war correspondent he saw the Battle of Britain From his experiences he wrote The Wounded Don't Cry and London Diary. When French reg-

ulations once threatened to prevent him from going to the front, he is said to have composed a cable to "Uncle Franklin" at the White House, signing it, "Your loving nephew, Quent." He got to the front.

Since 1941, he has written just about a book a year One of them, Courtroom, is the biography of Judge Samuel Leibowitz He is a big burly New Yorker, with reddish hair and a hearty appetite for life—which latter has helped make him the great reporter he is.

A New Look from Borrowed Time

BY RALPH RICHMOND

JUST TEN YEARS AGO I sat across the desk from a doctoi with a stethoscope. "Yes," he said, "theie is a lesion in the left upper lobe You have a moderately advanced case. . . ." I listened, stunned, as he continued. "You'll have to give up work at once and go to bed. Later on, we'll see. . ." He gave me no assurance.

Feeling like a man who, in mid-career, has suddenly been placed under sentence of death with an indefinite reprieve. I left the doctor's office, walked over to the park and sat down on a bench—perhaps, as I then told myself, for the last time. I needed to think.

In the next three days I cleared up my affairs. Then I went home, got into bed and set my watch to tick off not the minutes but the months.

Two and a half years, and many dashed hopes later, I left my bed and began the long climb back. It was another year before I made it.

I speak of this experience because these years that passed so slowly taught me what to value and what to believe. They said to me: Take time before time takes you.

I realize now that this world I'm living in is not my oyster to be opened, but my opportunity to be grasped. Each day to me is a precious entity. The sun comes up and presents me with twenty-four brand-new, wonderful hours—not to pass but to fill. I've learned to appreciate those little all-important things I never thought I had the time to notice before—the play of light on running water, the music of the wind in my favorite pine tree

I seem now to see and hear and feel with some of the recovered freshness of childhood. How well, for instance, I recall the touch of the springy earth under my feet the day I first stepped upon it after the years in bed. It was almost more than I could bear. It was like regaining one's citizenship in a world one had nearly lost.

Frequently I sit back and say to myself. Let me make note of this

149

moment I'm living right now. Because in it I'm well, happy, hard at work doing what I like best to do. It won't always be like this, so while it is, I'll make the most of it And afterwards, I'll remember and be grateful.

All this I owe to that long time spent "on the sidelines" of life. Wiser people come to this awareness without having to acquire it the hard way. But I wasn't wise enough. I'm wiser now—a little—and happier.

"Look thy last on all things lovely—every hour!" With these words Walter de la Mare sums up for me my philosophy and my belief. God made this world—in spite of what man now and then tries to do to un-make it—a dwelling-place of beauty and wonder, and He filled it with more goodness than most of us suspect And so I say to myself· Should I not pretty often take time to absorb the beauty and the wonder . . to contribute at least a little to the goodness? And should I not then, in my heart, give thanks? Truly I do. This I believe.

◆§ RALPH RICHMOND, poet and author, leads a busy nine-to-five life as a senior copywriter with a large national advertising agency Although his forte is verse and the essay, he was a prize winner in the Saturday Review of Literature's contest for a conclusion to Joseph Conrad's last, unfinished novel, Suspense He has also written much for children

Mr. Richmond's studies at the School of Journalism, Columbia University, were interrupted by World War I and a tour of duty in the Navy. He has traveled extensively in Europe and the Near East, but today lives quietly with Mrs. Richmond in an old, remodeled cottage in Bucks County.

He computes his output of words at several millions. However, he says that he can bear to reread but a few hundred without wincing Of the kind of man he is, the experience he relates above tells much.

Free Minds and Hearts at Work

BY JACKIE ROBINSON

AT THE BEGINNING of the World Series of 1947, I experienced a completely new emotion, when the National Anthem was played. This time, I thought, it is being played for me, as much as for anyone else. This is organized major league baseball, and I am standing here with all the others; and everything that takes place includes me.

About a year later, I went to Atlanta, Georgia, to play in an exhibition game. On the field, for the first time in Atlanta, there were Negroes and whites. Other Negroes, besides me. And I thought: What I have always believed has come to be.

And what is it that I have always believed? First, that imperfections are human. But that wherever human beings were given room to breathe and time to think, those imperfections would disappear, no matter how slowly. I do not believe that we have found or even approached perfection. That is not necessarily in the scheme of human events. Handicaps, stumbling blocks, prejudices—all of these are imperfect. Yet, they have to be reckoned with because they are in the scheme of human events.

Whatever obstacles I found made me fight all the harder. But it would have been impossible for me to fight at all, except that I was sustained by the personal and deep-rooted belief that my fight had a chance It had a chance because it took place in a free society. Not once was I forced to face and fight an immovable object. Not once was the situation so cast-iron rigid that I had no chance at all. Free minds and human hearts were at work all around me, and so there was the probability of improvement. I look at my children now, and know that I must still prepare them to meet obstacles and prejudices.

But I can tell them, too, that they will never face some of these prejudices because other people have gone before them. And to myself I can say that, because progress is unalterable, many of today's dogmas will have vanished by the time they grow into adults. I can

151

say to my children: There is a chance for you. No guarantee, but a chance. And this chance has come to be, because there is nothing static with free people There is no Middle Ages logic so strong that it can stop the human tide from flowing forward. I do not believe that every person, in every walk of life, can succeed in spite of any handicap. That would be perfection. But I do believe—and with every fiber in me—that what I was able to attain came to be because we put behind us (no matter how slowly) the dogmas of the past: to discover the truth of today, and perhaps find the greatness of tomorrow.

I believe in the human race.

I believe in the warm heart.

I believe in man's integrity.

I believe in the goodness of a free society.

And I believe that the society can remain good only as long as we are willing to fight for it—and to fight against whatever imperfections may exist.

My fight was against the barriers that kept Negroes out of baseball This was the area where I found imperfection, and where I was best able to fight. And I fought because I knew it was not doomed to be a losing fight.

It couldn't be a losing fight—not when it took place in a free society.

And, in the largest sense, I believe that what I did was done for me—that it was my faith in God that sustained me in my fight. And that what was done for me must and will be done for others.

⋘ JACKIE ROBINSON, great Negro baseball player, was born in Cairo, Georgia, and raised in Pasadena, California He attended Pasadena Junior College and the University of California at Los Angeles A football star at UCLA, he averaged a gain of twelve yards every time he carried the ball. He had to leave college in order to support his family

He was playing professional football with the Los Angeles Bulldogs when he was drafted into the Army in 1942.

Serving overseas, he won a commission. After the war, he played minor league baseball until he was offered a contract with the Brooklyn Dodgers

After a highly successful year with a Brooklyn "farm" team, Jackie made his first appearance with the Dodgers in 1947 and was voted the "Rookie of the Year" He is today one of the mainstays of "dem bums," and, quite properly, an inspiration to millions of youngsters. During baseball's off-season, he lives in Los Angeles.

My Faith Is Like a Circle

BY ANNE M. ROMBEAU

AMELIA EARHART once wrote· "Courage is the price that Life exacts for granting Peace." To me, courage is the act of living one's beliefs.

THIS I BELIEVE! That running through all nature, all races and the universe is the Divine Principle of Life. This Divine Principle—called God—animates all of us. It is like a circle whose center is everywhere, whose circumference is nowhere! My oneness with nature is best experienced as I walk, alone, in my garden when the dew is still clinging to the camellia, the violet, the rose. Better yet, I live this oneness with nature as I fly, alone in my plane, into the sunrise, high in limitless space, and into the embrace of stillness, peace and God! My oneness with races is felt most keenly in my at-homeness with Siberian Eskimos, Peruvian Indians or Chinese coolies. By contrast, I have found this oneness in dining at the Waldorf or talking with diplomats at embassies abroad. We are all human beings, all ONE, each individual trying in his own environment to live honestly, while preparing for a better future

THIS I BELIEVE! The Bible says: "As a man thinketh in his heart, so is he." The fact that man was given the power of choice makes it possible for him to control his own destiny. Those who have used that power have found peace.

Personally, I am thinking of the time fifteen years ago when my doctors pronounced me an invalid for life "A heart," they said, "does not rebuild at your age." Give up travel? Teaching? And, above all, flying? No! So, aware of the power which is within me, I simply drew upon it. Since that time, I have served my country for more than four years, first as civilian head of a flight school for the Navy and then as an officer in the Army Air Corps.

I have taught history, and history has taught me that basic, ethical principles have always been known to mankind; we have only developed and perfected them. Also, history has convinced me that each individual has contributed his cultural bit to a rivulet which has, in turn, commingled with a larger stream which has eventually been buffeted, swirled and finally merged into the ocean of present-day life. Each generation, each civilization has seen a better world. Yes, even in THESE TIMES—which I am painfully aware of because I am living through them—even in these times great constructive movements are glowing in power and strength. I see arising a unity of people, regardless of race or creed. This convinces me that world peace is an achievable, practical idea through the United Nations. To me the Principle of Life is universal and I believe that as individuals we control our destinies. So we can, in turn, control the destiny of the world When each of us is at peace with the best in self, when all of us will work for the best of all—then we will have world peace! We simply need courage.

To me, courage is the act of living one's beliefs.

◄§ ANNE ROMBEAU is a dynamic lecturer on contemporary problems, a world traveler, and a veteran aviatrix. Having earned her Master's degree in Social Sciences from Occidental College, she studied in France, Mexico, Argentina, and the Orient toward her Ph.D. In her travels she has used almost every form of transportation burro, camel, car, rail, ship and plane.

During the last war she was in charge of a Flight School for the Navy at Prescott, Arizona, and later was an officer in the Army Air Corps at Stewart Field, West Point. A past commander of the Amelia Earhart Post of the American Legion, she opened a memorial to the famed flier at the Smithsonian Institution, Washington, D C. In 1951 and 1952 she trail-blazed the All-Woman Transcontinental Air Race

A smiling, witty woman, she now lives on what she styles her "California ranch of one acre" and raises camellias, her favorite flower.

Growth That Starts from Thinking

BY MRS. ELEANOR ROOSEVELT

IT SEEMS TO ME a very difficult thing to put into words the beliefs we hold and what they make you do in your life. I think I was fortunate because I grew up in a family where there was a very deep religious feeling. I don't think it was spoken of a great deal. It was more or less taken for granted that everybody held certain beliefs and needed certain reinforcements of their own strength and that that came through your belief in God and your knowledge of prayer.

But as I grew older I questioned a great many of the things that I knew very well my grandmother who had brought me up had taken for granted And I think I might have been quite a difficult person to live with if it hadn't been for the fact that my husband once said it didn't do you any harm to learn those things, so why not let your children learn them? When they grow up they'll think things out for themselves.

And that gave me a feeling that perhaps that's what we all must do —think out for ourselves what we could believe and how we could live by it. And so I came to the conclusion that you had to use this life to develop the very best that you could develop.

I don't know whether I believe in a future life. I believe that all that you go through here must have some value, therefore there must be some reason. And there must be some "going on." How exactly that happens I've never been able to decide. There is a future—that I'm sure of. But how, that I don't know. And I came to feel that it didn't really matter very much because whatever the future held you'd have to face it when you came to it, just as whatever life holds you have to face it in exactly the same way. And the important thing was that you never let down doing the best that you were able to do— it might be poor because you might not have very much within you to give, or to help other people with, or to live your life with. But as long as you did the very best that you were able to do, then that was what you were put here to do and that was what you were accomplishing by being here.

And so I have tried to follow that out—and not to worry about the future or what was going to happen. I think I am pretty much of a fatalist. You have to accept whatever comes and the only important thing is that you meet it with courage and with the best that you have to give.

◄§ MRS. ELEANOR ROOSEVELT has never attended college, but she has received honorary degrees from a host of American, European and Asian universities. Known to millions through her newspaper columns and radio broadcasts, she is tall and impressive-looking and fairly exudes good health and good will.

During World War II, she worked in the Office of Civilian Defense. She also made trips to Great Britain, the South Pacific, New Zealand, Australia, and the Caribbean to visit our servicemen. Undoubtedly she is the best-traveled First Lady in our history.

Mrs. Roosevelt has been a delegate to every General Assembly of the United Nations. In the United States she is a member of the Human Rights Commission, having served as its chairman continuously until 1951 Her one and only hobby is people Despite her vast responsibilities, she calls herself quite simply and modestly "an average housewife."

Don't Step Out of Character

BY VIRGINIA SALE

ON A PLANE flying from Chicago to New York, my seat companion was a young girl who gave me a friendly smile as I sat beside her, but whose young face showed great sadness. Hesitantly, she told me she was on her way to the funeral of her seventeen-year-old brother, who had been killed in Korea. She also told me that her only other relatives were two brothers, both in the service, and that they had lost their eldest brother in the war in Europe. I wanted to say something to comfort her . . . I felt so useless. . . . All I could say was "I'm so sorry." And I thought, "Just what can I do to help bring order and hope into the world today?" And the thought came to me, "I can pray and my prayers will tune in with other sincere prayers to create a mighty force for good and for peace in the world."

As a girl I was fortunate in having old-fashioned, religious parents, and I often think of the old hymn my good father sang so lustily as I stood beside him in church, "I need Thee every hour." As I've grown older my philosophy has changed—in a way. I don't think of God now as an old man with a long gray beard sitting up on a throne. I believe in a practical religion. What good is it unless I can use it to help solve my daily problems, large or small?

I am grateful for what I consider the most worthwhile things in my life—a happy marriage, a good husband, and a son and daughter who become infinitely finer as they grow up. Success in my theatrical career has come second to these. However, no matter what my material blessings may be, I realize that my happiness must come from within myself. I can't get back anything I don't give out. Anybody knows a sure cure for the blues is to get out and do something nice for someone else.

I have had a wonderful opportunity, on my tours with my one-woman show, to meet fine, good people in every one of the seven

157

hundred towns I've played. From them I know that good people predominate in every part of this country.

I love my work. I believe that laughter is a great soul cleanser, and I pray that my audiences may somehow be better off for having seen my show. I believe in blessing everything and everybody along the way. Sometimes I may have let stage fright and nerves rob me and my audience of my best performance. I have failed if I haven't beforehand blessed everyone in my audience, everyone backstage, and, when I'm working in television, radio or motion pictures, everyone in the studio—my fellow actors and the director and technicians I admire their courage, their goodhearted generous qualities.

What do I mean by "blessing"? Well, I first have a deep sense of gratitude to an audience, and a feeling of good will and good wishes, so that I know there is complete harmony between them and me, and I know they will like me because I really like them—that we will tune in together.

My late brother, the great character actor and comedian, Charles "Chic" Sale, said to me one time we were talking about spiritual things and about being perfect channels for expression: "The thing to do, kiddo, is to stay in character—be God's child." And I try never to forget this.

◄§ VIRGINIA SALE leads a busy life as a versatile and hard-working character actress. Ranked by critics with Ruth Draper and Cornelia Otis Skinner, she has toured countless cities in her original one-woman show entitled Americana. Audiences have seen her in three hundred Hollywood movies, as well as in other phases of show business.

She and her brother, the famed Chic Sale, both trace their talent to a long line of circuit-riding preachers. Born in Urbana, Illinois, she attended the University of Illinois and the American Academy of Dramatic Arts. Now living in New York City, she is married to director Sam Wren, and has sixteen-year-old twins, Ginny and Christopher Wren. Besides acting, she writes, a book of her monologues has just been published. She is also active in philanthropic work. With it all, she calls herself "just a small-town girl." Her humor is kindly and never biting, because it is based on an understanding of and a sympathy for her fellow man.

I Do a Lot of Office Fishing

BY RICHARD SALMON

SOME YEARS AGO I started to look at the stars through high-powered binoculars, and began reading in books written by astronomers for people like me. I became an entranced star-gazer for a while.

The men who have learned as much as we know about the universe point out that the sun is an insignificant, moderately hot star in the nebula where it is fixed. The Milky Way, which I have always wanted to spell "w-h-e-y," is composed of our brothers and sisters, and we are all moving around a central hub; and the hub is moving toward some place; I don't know where. My brothers and sisters are numbered in billions of billions and our galaxy itself is one of many, many . . . how many I don't know.

Our sun is so small and our earth, its offspring, is so tiny that when I think of the magnitude, I think of what O. Henry described as a "Statue of What's the Use."

What difference does it make that I exist? What possible influence can I make, or my nation make, or my world make?

Where am I going on this ride and does it make any sense? Who's the boss and what's He got in mind?

That's what I got to thinking . . . it's all too big, too inevitable, too uncontrollable, and if I think about it with my eyes closed, it's a pretty pessimistic picture.

Then one day I saw a hunting dog in the woods, an English setter flecked with black. His tail was tangled with dock burs. This is a common occurrence to guys like me. I always want to stop and pull out the burs. But this time, out of nowhere, came the realization that this bounding, healthy dog was performing an important job: the job of transporting seeds that were constructed for the very purpose of hitch-hiking. The fluff of milkweed sails on the wind to start a new colony miles from its original parent; this dog and his tangle of dock burs are all part of a plan. And so am I.

I believe the plan on this small, lonely earth is to make the best of it—a policy that is becoming increasingly more difficult as the number of human beings increases.

When I came to New York many years ago, I found that in big cities people live faster and decide things quicker than country folk. They have to, in order to survive in the struggle for existence.

Several times a week I slug it out with city dwellers for a place in the subway. They seem to be a bad lot. But when I pass a city dweller on a trout stream I find he's just like other people. He'll speak to me with interest, even warmth. He will ask me how many trout I've taken, what fly was successful, and I break down and tell him, and point out that perhaps the black gnat he is using is too large.

I have tried to make the best of it by doing a lot of office fishing, some front porch fishing, and some quiet mulling about the magnificent things like dock burs and remote stars. What's more, I have found it fun; fun that has brought me a lot of happiness, a lot of contentment and a lot of peace.

◆§ RICHARD SALMON, artist and author, was born in the hunting and fishing country of central Pennsylvania. Although he is by profession a designer in the graphic arts in New York, he excelled in biology at Washington and Jefferson College, and this interest is apparent in his present-day hobbies, which include hunting and fishing. A leading artificial fly tier, his collection of dry flies and the materials used in their construction was exhibited at the American Museum of Natural History.

His book, *Fly Fishing for Trout*, is considered a definitive work.

Mr Salmon lives in Snedens Landing, on the Hudson, in an old house full of Audubon pictures, rods, reels, and trout flies. His is the philosophy of the naturalist who observes all types of animals—two-legged, four-legged, and otherwise. His conclusion, based upon observed phenomena, is that in what may seem to be a disordered world, everything is in reality going according to plan.

Suffering Is Self-Manufactured

BY DR. LEON J. SAUL

I BELIEVE the immediate purpose of life is to live—to survive All known forms of life go through life cycles. The basic plan is: birth —maturing—mating—reproducing—death

Thus the immediate purpose of human life is for each individual to fulfill his life cycle This involves proper maturing into the fully developed adult of the specie.

The pine tree grows straight unless harmful influences warp it. So does the human being. It is a finding of the greatest significance that the mature man and woman have the nature and characteristics of the good spouse and parent: the ability to enjoy responsible working and loving

If the world consisted primarily of mature persons—loving, responsible, productive, toward family, friends and the world—most of our human problems would be resolved.

But most people have suffered in childhood from influences which have warped their development. Hence, as adults they have not realized their full and proper nature. They feel something is wrong without knowing what it is. They feel inferior, frustrated, insecure, and anxious And they react to these inner feelings just as any animal reacts to any hurt or threat. by readiness to fight or to flee. Flight carries them into alcoholism and other mental disorders. Fight impels them to crime, cruelty, war.

This readiness to violence, this inhumanity of man to man, is the basic problem of human life—for, in the form of war, it now threatens to extinguish us.

Without the fight-flight reaction, man would never have survived the cave and the jungle. But now, through social living, man has made himself relatively safe from the elements and wild beasts. He is even learning to protect himself against disease. He can produce adequate food, clothing and shelter for the present population of the earth. Barring a possible astronomical accident, he now faces no serious threat to his existence, except one—the fight-flight reaction within himself. This jungle readiness to hurt and to kill is now a vestigial hangover like the appendix, which interferes with the new and more powerful means of coping with nature through civilization Trying to solve every problem by fighting or fleeing is the primitive method, still central for the immature child. The later method, understanding and co-operation, requires the mature capacities of the adult In an infantile world, fighting may be forced upon one. Then it is more effective if handled maturely for mature goals. Probably war will cease only when enough people are mature.

The basic problem is social adaptation and biologic survival. The basic solution is for people to understand the nature of their own biological emotional maturity, to work toward it, to help the children in their development toward it.

Human suffering is mostly made by man himself It is primarily the result of the failure of adults, because of improper child-rearing, to mature emotionally. Hence instead of enjoying their capacities for responsible work and love, they are grasping, egocentric, insecure, frustrated, anxious and hostile.

Maturity is the path from madness and murder to inner peace and satisfying living for each individual and for the human specie

This I believe on the evidence of science and through personal observation and experience.

◄§ DR LEON J. SAUL, who holds degrees from Columbia and Harvard, is professor of clinical psychiatry at the University of Pennsylvania School of Medicine. He is a slight man of perhaps deceptively frail appearance whose penetrating, though not unkindly, eyes peer at you from behind shell-rimmed glasses He lives in a big, old-fashioned farmhouse outside Media, Pennsylvania.

During World War II he was in charge of the combat fatigue program at the Philadelphia Naval Base, with the rank of commander.

Author of two recent and important books on psychoanalysis—*Emotional Maturity* and *Bases of Human Behavior*—Dr Saul terms himself a "professional understander." His philosophy, he declares, is drawn from the life around him, events and people, mostly the latter, and, as he proves above, he believes the way to happiness and well-being lies in the understanding of men's minds.

I Never Stopped Believing

BY EVA R. SAXL

I BELIEVE that it is important to be brought up with a firm belief in the good. I was fortunate in this respect. My parents not only gave me a happy home, but they had me study half a dozen foreign languages, and made it possible for me to travel in other countries. This made me more tolerant and helped me to bridge many difficulties in later life

Soon after I had married, my husband and I left our native Czechoslovakia and went to live in Shanghai, China. Here was a really international city. People of all races and creeds lived and worked together As everywhere, there were good and bad people. I found out that most people are kind and good. But in the Orient one cannot always be certain. Many people do not show their true character openly. Often it is difficult to strike the chord that will get a harmonious response. But when we spoke Chinese, we could strike these chords. In return, the Chinese taught us much about their philosophy of life.

In Shanghai, in 1941, when I was only twenty years old, the doctors discovered that I had diabetes It was a terrible shock, because diabetes is incurable. But it can be controlled by insulin. Although this drug was not manufactured in China, there were ample stocks of imported insulin available. This enabled me to continue a normal, happy life

Then bombs fell on Pearl Harbor and the Japanese occupied Shanghai The import of insulin was cut off. Before long there was not enough for the diabetics. I was on a starvation diet, to keep my insulin requirements as low as possible. But my meager supplies soon scraped bottom. Many diabetics had already died and the situation became desperate. Throughout all of it, I never stopped believing that with the help of God and my husband's love and care I would survive.

I continued to teach in Chinese schools. My faith and my husband's never-ending effort to get the manufacture of insulin started gave me courage. Buffalo pancreas was secured and in a small laboratory the production of insulin was attempted. I served as the human guinea pig on which it was tested. I'll never forget the day when my husband gave me the first injection of the new insulin, which had worked on rabbits. It helped! Can you imagine our happiness and relief?

But there were still other things to worry about. Tropical diseases, inflation and the Japanese military. Oh yes, also American B-29s. Once they hit the power plant and cut off our electricity. Without it, no insulin could be made. These were difficult times indeed!

Besides my trust in God, I derived the greatest strength from the deep love and complete understanding between my husband and me. And next to that was the kindness and help of many, many friends of many nationalities. Even some Japanese civilians, although their country was at war with us, helped, whenever they could.

To me, who lived under enemy occupation, freedom has a special meaning. My dreams came true when we were sailing towards the United States, where life, liberty and the pursuit of happiness are the rights of every human being.

Therefore this country—of people from many lands—has so quickly become my cherished home. In it, I believe.

◆§ EVA R. SAXL is a blonde, vivacious young lady born in Prague, Czechoslovakia After attending a Czech grammar school, German and French high schools, and an English college, she rounded out her knowledge of half a dozen languages by studying Italian and Spanish. She married at nineteen and ever since then her life has revolved around the love and understanding that she and her husband have for each other.

When they settled in Shanghai, China, they both added to their linguistic equipment through the study of Chinese. Eva Saxl loves to travel and has covered most of Europe, Asia, and North America. Her personal impressions, adventures, and sense of humor combine to make her a resourceful writer and lecturer.

Now a grateful and proud American, she believes that by making friends with people of other nationalities, and by talking to them in their own language, one can help to break down the barriers that have too long existed between nations.

The World's Greatest Force

BY DORE SCHARY

WHAT WE BELIEVE is usually the result of what we have lived—and it is difficult to synopsize forty-six years of living and believing in six hundred words, but these things I do believe:

Having been reared in a religious home and having known many people of sincere and deep religious convictions of many faiths, I believe in God and in prayer. I believe in the Ten Commandments —and since obedience to the law is a deep factor in the Jewish faith, I believe conscientiously in law and order.

Being the son of immigrant parents who found opportunity and security in America, and having been a student of our history, I believe deeply in America and its conscience and philosophy. I believe that our republic has operated for a longer time with more good for most people than any other government in history—and so I believe in democracy, and view any kind of totalitarianism as a dangerous threat and a menace.

Having been happily married for twenty years and blessed with three children, I have firm convictions about the family unit and its effect on the human spirit. Since love and understanding form the keystone of the family unit, and since our society is actually an extension of the family unit spreading from the family to the neighborhood to the city to the state to the nation—and hopefully one day to the world—I most sincerely believe in love and understanding.

Having enjoyed the friendship of many people in many places for many years, I believe in the innate dignity of the individual and have learned that, in the main, people are as we choose to find them; that reason can overcome prejudice; that knowledge can overcome ignorance; that love can overcome hate; and that goodness can conquer evil.

Finally, I believe that in our temporal world, the greatest force that can operate for the best interests of all is the cleansing and

165

strengthening force of wisdom, without which man would still be living in caves—slightly removed from the beasts whose skins he would wear to cover himself. Wisdom has given us our homes, our factories and dams—our medicine and our automobiles—our toys and our weapons—our subways and our planes—our books and our radio—our motion pictures and our television. Wisdom has given us our faith—and wisdom brings us hope and trust in the future, along with pride in our past. With wisdom we flourish and live. Without it we wither and die With wisdom years can keep us young in heart and mind. Without it we grow old. With wisdom we can be strong and know no fear. Without it we become weak and frightened.

These things I believe—not alone because I choose them, but primarily because I have lived them—and living is believing.

DORE SCHARY, Vice-President in charge of production and studio operations at Metro-Goldwyn-Mayer in Culver City, California, is a big, hard working, brilliant, but amiable man whom somebody once described as looking like an indulgent uncle

A man of monumental patience, he seems to have come by this quality as a result of the variety of his past occupations. His varied career also probably accounts for his interest in furthering brotherhood and good will among men. He is noted for his work in support of Boys Town.

Among his best known pictures are *Boys Town*, *Young Tom Edison*, *Bataan* and *Battleground*. He is co-author of *Case History of a Movie*, a definitive book on the motion picture. As a showman, he works with this formula, which has already brought him an Academy Award: Entertain but edify.

Closer Than My Own Back Yard

BY WILLIAM B. SEARS

I REMEMBER once doing a television broadcast from a Philadelphia hospital. It featured a contest among the children who had been born there during the past several years. The winner was a three-year-old boy. As the gold cup was presented to him, we took a "close-up." He grasped the cup eagerly with both hands and raised it up to his lips to drink from it. Surprised he lowered it and tearfully cried out: "It's empty!"

It made me think how many times all of us have tilted proffered cups hoping for assurance only to find them empty, too. The more I talk with my fellow man, the more I realize that my hopes are their hopes. That, as eagerly as I, they search for sort of a "holy grail" whose contents can nourish all mankind.

I'm beginning to understand the wisdom of Bacon's words: "If we are to transform the world, we must begin first by transforming ourselves." At the same time I have come to realize that like the search for Maeterlinck's well-known bluebird, happiness is not a matter of geography. I think it is found even closer than my own back yard—within myself. It was a long struggle for me to understand that actually no one loved me. Not my father, mother, wife, or children. I believe that nobody loves you either. What I mean is that people love the qualities that you possess—kindness, understanding, justice. As you add these qualities to your life, their love for you increases; as you lose these qualities, their love for you falls away. What is true of individuals, I think, is true of nations. Respect, allegiance, and devotion are won by moral character. This character can be acquired by men or countries only through a fundamental belief in some great ruling force which can give purpose to their lives. It is no longer unpopular or unscientific to believe in God.

Anyone who lives in the sports world, for instance, recognizes the vital need for authority and an overseeing guidance. When this law

167

of order and authority is traced back to its source, it leads finally and inevitably to a belief in God. To me, this is the only true basis for a peaceful and happy life.

True, this Supreme Being may be beyond my definition or description, yet this tremendous force which has been released to the world through all the great religions is a positive thing, I feel, and creates life.

Humbly, before this force, I believe in meditation and prayer. But I believe in active living, too. I believe that I owe it to myself to extract all the throbbing wonder, joy, and thrill out of life—from my profession, from music, the sciences, art, from all created things. In a wonderful, intimate way, the world is mine to fulfill the promise that lies within me I need only remember one thing: nothing must come between me and my responsibilities to God and my fellow man

Glory is not his who loves his country, his family, or himself alone; glory is his who loves his kind. This, I believe, has helped me to look upon each dawn as a new adventure, a day wherein I may find the cup that is not empty

WILLIAM B. SEARS is a seventy-five-year-old philosopher every Sunday on the CBS television program *In the Park*, and a forty-one-year-old humorist the other six days of the week on his radio program over Station WCAU in Philadelphia Mr. Sears ("Bill" to millions) maintains that his career has progressed in direct proportion to the disappearance of his hair. Through the years he has been a sportscaster, correspondent for the United Press, and radio director for an advertising agency.

When he is not writing his radio or television programs, he paints in water colors and in oils. The rest of his spare time is devoted to repairing the damage that two hundred years have done to his old frame farmhouse in Chester County, Pennsylvania.

As chairman of the National Radio Committee for the Bahai World Faith, Mr. Sears spends much time in writing and speaking for all groups on the vital need for a return to "spiritual values."

Personal Inventory by Appointment

BY LOUIS B. SELTZER

EACH DAY I have a special appointment.

Unfailingly, I have kept it, since a small boy.

I intend to keep it every day for the rest of my life.

I meet my God.

With His help, I take an inventory of myself, just before I release my mind to sleep.

The measure by which He and I judge me is simple.

It is a blunt, searching, severe inventory.

It covers thoughts, and acts, and impulses, and temptations, and even tentative inclinations.

In what respects have you failed? What thoughts had you that were not good? What man did you ignore? Were you completely honorable in all you did that day?

I believe God gives us something to begin with.

It is not much. In my case, I know it was not much. I am not sure today it is much.

It is, however, up to me, with God's help, to fashion myself of that clay, and those chemicals, and that tentative personality, and that spirit, into something approximating what He would like me to be.

In my wallet I have three pieces of paper. They are yellowed and frayed I refer to them constantly.

One says: "What doth the Lord require of thee, but to do justly, and to love mercy, and to walk humbly with Thy God."

Did I do so that day?

Another says: "I expect to pass through this world but once. Any good therefore that I can do, or any kindness that I can show to any fellow creature, let me do it now. Let me not defer or neglect it, for I shall not pass this way again."

Did I measure up to that—this day?

Another says: "Make big plans, aim high in hope and work, remembering that a noble, logical diagram once recorded will never die."

At the end of the day, in communion with God—what of that?

I believe, profoundly, that each of us has a mission to perform so long as he lives.

It is to take the foundation God gives us at birth, and make of it, by discipline, such light as we let into our soul, such reason as we cultivate by maturing our minds with the good thoughts and distilled wisdom of others, and our own; by consciously lifting ourselves to the spiritual summits achieved by God and His good people—thus to make and strengthen ourselves so that in our time on this troubled planet we will have given to it something more than just our labor, and our material accomplishments—something that can be measured as good in the sight of our God.

◄§ Louis B. Seltzer (his associates would not dream of ever calling him anything more formal than "Louie") is editor of the Scripps-Howard Cleveland Press.

"Balding" is one of his favorite self-descriptions—possibly a slight understatement. Dapper, boy-faced, he is usually to be found in the City Room rather than in his private office.

He is one of Cleveland's first citizens, and belongs to just about every club in town. He is always in great demand for civic drives and as a speaker. Co-founder of the American Press Institute at Columbia University, in 1951 he received the award of the National Conference of Christians and Jews for his thirty years spent in promoting better relations among all races and religions. He and Mrs. Seltzer live in a suburb of Cleveland, in a house "fashionable enough," he says, "to have been 'burgled' recently." They have two children and five grandchildren.

A Reporter Quotes His Sources

By WILLIAM L. SHIRER

It's RATHER DIFFICULT in these noisy, confusing, nerve-racking days to achieve the peace of mind in which to pause for a moment to reflect on what you believe in. There's so little time and opportunity to give it much thought—though it is the thing we live by; and without it, without beliefs, human existence today would hardly be bearable.

My own view of life, like everyone else's, is conditioned by personal experience. In my own case, there were two experiences, in particular, which helped to shape my beliefs: years of life and work under a totalitarian regime, and a glimpse of war.

Living in a totalitarian land taught me to value highly—and fiercely —the very things the dictators denied· tolerance, respect for others and, above all, the freedom of the human spirit.

A glimpse of war filled me with wonder not only at man's courage and capacity for self-sacrifice, but at his stubborn, marvelous will to preserve, to endure, to prevail—amidst the most incredible savagery and suffering. When you saw people—civilians—who were bombed out, or who, worse, had been hounded in the concentration camps or worked to a frazzle in the slave-labor gangs—when you saw them come out of these ordeals of horror and torture, still intact as human beings, with a will to go on, with a faith still in themselves, in their fellow man and in God, you realized that man was indestructible. You appreciated, too, that despite the corruption and cruelty of life, man somehow managed to retain great virtues: love, honor, courage, self-sacrifice, compassion.

It filled you with a certain pride just to be a member of the human race. It renewed your belief in your fellow men.

Of course, there are many days (in this Age of Anxiety) when a human being feels awfully low and discouraged. I myself find consolation at such moments by two means. trying to develop a sense of history, and renewing the quest for an inner life.

I go back, for example, to reading Plutarch. He reminds you that even in the golden days of Greece and Rome, from which so much that is splendid in our own civilization derives, there was a great deal of what we find so loathsome in life today war, strife, corruption, treason, double-crossing, intolerance, tyranny, rabble-rousing. Reading history thus gives you perspective. It enables you to see your troubles relatively. You don't take them so seriously then.

Finally, I find that most true happiness comes from one's inner life, from the disposition of the mind and soul. Admittedly, a good inner life is difficult to achieve, especially in these trying times. It takes reflection and contemplation. And self-discipline. One must be honest with oneself, and that's not easy. (You have to have patience and understanding. And, when you can, seek God)

But the reward of having an inner life, which no outside storm or evil turn of fortune can touch, is, it seems to me, a very great one.

WILLIAM L. SHIRER, foreign correspondent and radio commentator, is the author of Berlin Diary, End of a Berlin Diary, Midcentury Journey, and a novel, The Traitor. A recipient of both earned and honorary degrees from Coe College, Iowa, his awards include the Peabody Award in Radio, the Wendell Willkie One World Award, and the Legion of Honor

In 1925 he went abroad for two months and stayed for more than two decades Paris, London, Vienna, Berlin, Rome, and Spain were some of the places where his assignments called him. He had the unusual experience of being bombed in Berlin by the British and bombed in London by the Germans.

His latest book, Midcentury Journey, was written during the midcentury year. Notes for it were scribbled in many places: on a plane over the ocean, in Salzburg, Paris, Bonn, London, and all over the United States. The book itself was written in his apartment in New York and at his farm in Connecticut

Everything Potent Is Dangerous

BY WALLACE STEGNER

IT IS TERRIBLY DIFFICULT to say honestly, without posing or faking, what one truly and fundamentally believes. Reticence or an itch to make public confession may distort or dramatize what is really there to be said, and public expressions of belief are so closely associated with inspirational activity, and in fact so often stem from someone's desire to buck up the downhearted and raise the general morale, that belief becomes an evangelical matter.

In all honesty, what I believe is neither inspirational nor evangelical. Passionate faith I am suspicious of because it hangs witches and burns heretics, and generally I am more in sympathy with the witches and heretics than with the sectarians who hang and burn them. I fear immoderate zeal, Christian, Moslem, Communist, or whatever, because it restricts the range of human understanding and the wise reconciliation of human differences, and creates an orthodoxy with a sword in its hand.

I cannot say that I am even a sound Christian, though the code of conduct to which I subscribe was preached more eloquently by Jesus Christ than by any other. About God I simply do not know; I don't think I can know.

However far I have missed achieving it, I know that moderation is one of the virtues I most believe in. But I believe as well in a whole catalogue of Christian and classical virtues: in kindness and generosity, in steadfastness and courage and much else. I believe further that good depends not on things but on the use we make of things. Everything potent, from human love to atomic energy, is dangerous; it produces ill about as readily as good; it becomes good only through the control, the discipline, the wisdom with which we use it. Much of this control is social, a thing which laws and institutions and uniforms enforce, but much of it must be personal, and I do not see how we can evade the obligation to take full responsibility

173

for what we individually do. Our reward for self-control and the acceptance of private responsibility is not necessarily money or power. Self-respect and the respect of others are quite enough

All this is to say that I believe in conscience, not as something implanted by divine act, but as something learned from infancy from the tradition and society which has bred us. The outward forms of virtue will vary greatly from nation to nation; a Chinese scholar of the old school, or an Indian raised on the Vedas and the *Bhagavad Gita*, has a conscience that will differ from mine. But in the essential outlines of what constitutes human decency we vary amazingly little. The Chinese and the Indian know as well as I do what kindness is, what generosity is, what fortitude is. They can define justice quite as accurately. It is only when they and I are blinded by tribal and denominational narrowness that we insist upon our differences and can recognize goodness only in the robes of our own crowd.

Man is a great enough creature and a great enough enigma to deserve both our pride and our compassion, and engage our fullest sense of mystery. I shall certainly never do as much with my life as I want to, and I shall sometimes fail miserably to live up to my conscience, whose word I do not distrust even when I can't obey it. But I am terribly glad to be alive; and when I have wit enough to think about it, terribly proud to be a man and an American, with all the rights and privileges that those words connote, and most of all I am humble before the responsibilities that are also mine. For no right comes without a responsibility, and being born luckier than most of the world's millions, I am also born more obligated.

◄§ WALLACE STEGNER is a teacher with one hand and a writer with the other. Professor of English at Stanford University, he directs its writing program, and in his "think house" in the hills behind the University he continues to produce books, stories, and articles. His novels include *The Big Rock Candy Mountain*, *Second Growth*, and *The Preacher and the Slave*.

His stories have appeared in magazines both here and abroad, some of them having been collected in the volume *The Woman on the Wall* His literary prizes include Houghton Mifflin's Life in America Award, the *Saturday Review's* Anisfield Wolfe Award, and three O. Henry Prizes for short stories

In 1950 Mr. Stegner and his wife spent seven months making a literary exploration of Asia. At present he is on a Guggenheim Fellowship, completing a biography of John Wesley Powell.

You Have to Water the Plant

BY LELAND STOWE

FOR THE THINGS I BELIEVE IN I must give a reporter's answer. Like everyone else, it's out of my own experience. For twenty-four years I've been up to my neck in the world's troubles . . . meeting people in dozens of foreign countries . . . watching other nations drift into war—and America too. It's convinced me that one of the most important things in life—for every one of us—is understanding . . . trying to see the other fellow's point of view. I've often thought—if I could really put myself in the other person's shoes, see things the way he sees them, feel what he feels, how much more tolerant and fair I'd be. I remember, back in the twenties, the bitter arguments between Europeans and Americans about reducing the war debts. I had to explain what the Europeans felt, and why. I learned then that there's almost always some right, and some wrong, on both sides. We didn't think enough about the Europeans' point of view. They didn't think enough about ours. When lack of understanding becomes pronounced, it leads to hatred and war. But it's like that in our daily life, too. If I talk disparagingly about any racial group, I promote hatred—dissension in our society. I haven't thought how I would feel if I belonged to that group. In Berlin I saw Hitler's thugs beating up helpless Jews. Then, back home, sometimes I heard people say: "Well, it's their affair." They forgot that freedom and fair play belong to all human beings—not to lucky Americans only. They forgot that people are *people*—of whatever creed, color or nationality. I remember the poor Spanish and Greek peasants who shared their bread and cheese with me—all they had! . . . The old Russian woman who made me take her bed, while she slept on the floor. . . . So many simple people who couldn't speak my language— but spoke with their hearts. One of the happiest things in my life is this. My best friends are like a roster of the United Nations—Europeans, Asians, Latin Americans, North Americans—just *people*,

175

from all over the world. The best part is discovering how much we have in common—the constant reminder that friendship has no national barriers—the knowledge that all kinds of people really can understand each other. We all have to live in this world. But we are all a mixture of good and bad. But I've found more of the good than the bad in most people—in every country. I think you only have to look Understanding is a flower blossoming. But you have to water the plant. Then, when it blossoms, what a wonderful feeling! You feel that way when you make a new friend. I guess understanding really is charity and love. I know it gives a new meaning to our lives. When I die I wish people might say: "He helped people to understand each other better." Of course, I often fail. But just trying makes living seem worth while.

⋄§ LELAND STOWE, born in Southbury, Connecticut, in 1899, has spent the past quarter of a century as a foreign correspondent, in peace and war, on five continents A Pulitzer prize winner for dispatches from Europe between the wars, he was correspondent with the armies of seven different nations and colonies in the last war.

His dispatches on the German occupation of Oslo and the British defeat in Norway have been cited as examples of war reporting at its best. He has written several best-sellers based on his world observations, his latest book, Conquest By Terror, is the story of satellite Europe.

His shock of white hair never concealed by a hat, the ebullient Mr. Stowe lives a life charged with energy, whether patrolling the Iron Curtain or between assignments at home in New York. His tastes run to exotic foods, fine wines, folk songs and the zestful companionship of international friends.

Attuning the Listening Ear

BY CHARLES P. TAFT

OCCASIONALLY in old speech notes I find a few persistent threads of ideas which I still use. Are these beliefs, or are they merely a crystallization of past preaching?

One of those ideas seems to me a basic premise of my beliefs. I must be ready to sift out from the expressions of others whatever may have come to them from God's inspiration. It is easy to spout; it is far harder to cultivate a truly listening ear.

The listening ear implies humility, for it assumes a readiness to accept upsetting new ideas. The listening ear in which I believe also implies an eagerness for participation of others, both in discussion and in action.

These qualities, the ear that listens with humility and the eagerness for participation of others, are the essential lubricants of our lives as social animals, in families, groups, communities, and all our organizations also represent a complete denial of absolutism in any form, including the hard-and-fast party line.

But how can one be humble and receptive, and yet have convictions that are worth anything?

There *is* one standard of absolute love, and I do have convictions about how it affects me. This is the spirit of God, a person of generous love and affection whose characteristics I can see in Jesus. For me God does no self-starting miracles while I sit quiescent, for He does His work only through people when we suffer or cause suffering, either through our own perversity, or ignorance or some unexplained residue of evil, and He suffers with us. Always He welcomes us and gives us free choices to come from us and we have to approach this with full understanding of how far short of His perfect ideal we have fallen. I think of God, therefore, as essentially democratic, seeking our participation in His love, not as an autocrat.

But I live usually on a level far below that, where I act by more matter-of-fact rules of thumb. I find in myself the desire to excel by hard work, which I try to make creative by using all my acquired know-how, and all the ingenuity I can muster, with a taking of risks that I try to calculate. That adds up to a determination not to be stopped by the usual obstructions, or the unusual ones either.

I try to find the tie between this commonplace and the sublime by subjecting these rules of thumb to God's standard of live and generous spirit

I try to test my course of action and my decisions by these refined rules of thumb. Every so often I stop to wonder whether the turning I took last year, or many years back, under the impulse of one of those incentives was the right turn. And I may occasionally get that sinky feeling at the pit of the stomach at the thought of where I go at death, quite irrespective of what turns I took.

But this fear of death, perhaps also the urge for personal salvation, seem to me essentially selfish, however natural and human. Our goal is the accomplishment of God's broad purpose in friendly souls working without haste and without rest. This I believe, and I believe in it above all for anyone who has had more than his share of God's blessings.

CHARLES P. TAFT was born in Cincinnati in 1897, the son of William Howard Taft, who became the twenty-seventh President. Now a distinguished lawyer, he lives in his native Cincinnati with his wife, Eleanor. They have six children and nine grandchildren.

At the outbreak of the First World War, he enlisted in the Army and served overseas, where he won a commission. Returning to this country, he enrolled in the law school at Yale. He played tackle on the University's championship football team and captained the basketball squad. After his graduation, and in association with his brother Robert, he formed the widely known law firm of Taft, Stettinius and Hollister.

For his contribution to the war effort during the Second World War, he received the Medal of Merit Active in many charities, he has been a national leader in the Community Chest. He is also a past president of the Federal Council of Churches.

Give Part of Yourself Away

BY DR. HAROLD TAYLOR

WE ARE LIVING in one of those periods in human history which are marked by revolutionary changes in all of man's ideas and values. It is a time when every one of us must look within himself to find what ideas, what beliefs, and what ideals each of us will live by. And unless we find these ideals, and unless we stand by them firmly, we have no power to overcome the crisis in which we in our world find ourselves.

I believe in people, in sheer, unadulterated humanity. I believe in listening to what people have to say, in helping them to achieve the things which they want and the things which they need. Naturally, there are people who behave like beasts, who kill, who cheat, who lie and who destroy. But without a belief in man and a faith in his possibilities for the future, there can be no hope for the future, but only bitterness that the past has gone. I believe we must, each of us, make a philosophy by which we can live. There are people who make a philosophy out of believing in nothing They say there is no truth, that goodness is simply cleverness in disguising your own selfishness. They say that life is simply the short gap in between an unpleasant birth and an inevitable death. There are others who say that man is born into evil and sinfulness and that life is a process of purification through suffering and that death is the reward for having suffered There are others who say that man is a kind of machine which operates according to certain laws, and that if you can learn the laws and seize the power to manipulate the machine. you can make man behave automatically to serve whatever ends you have in mind.

I believe these philosophies are false. The most important thing in life is the way it is lived, and there is no such thing as an abstract happiness, an abstract goodness or morality, or an abstract anything, except in terms of the person who believes and who acts. There is only the single human being who lives and who, through every

179

moment of his own personal living experience, is being happy or unhappy, noble or base, wise or unwise, or simply existing.

The question is: How can these individual moments of human experience be filled with the richness of a philosophy which can sustain the individual in his own life? Unless we give part of ourselves away, unless we can live with other people and understand them and help them, we are missing the most essential part of our own human lives. The fact that the native endowment of the young mind is one of liberalism and confidence in the powers of man for good is the basis of my philosophy. And if only man can be given a free chance to use his powers, this philosophy will result in a boundless flow of vital energy and a willingness to try new things, combined with a faith in the future.

There are as many roads to the attainment of wisdom and goodness as there are people who undertake to walk them. There are as many solid truths on which we can stand as there are people who can search them out and who will stand on them There are as many ideas and ideals as there are men of good will who will hold them in their minds and act them in their lives.

◄§ HAROLD TAYLOR became president of Sarah Lawrence College when he was thirty. Best known as a vigorous spokesman for liberal thinking about modern education, his opinions on intellectual freedom and experimental education have attracted wide attention Despite his busy administrative life, his early interests in philosophy, literature and the arts have remained alive and active.

Born in Canada, he earned two degrees from the University of Toronto and his Doctorate from the University of London. After a year of traveling and writing in Europe, he joined the philosophy department of the University of Wisconsin Here he coached the tennis team and played clarinet with the University orchestra, besides teaching a variety of stimulating courses.

"My advice to the young," says Dr. Taylor (himself still in his thirties), "is to work hard, listen hard, suspect all abstractions, develop a talent for detecting falsehood and a love for knowing and speaking the truth "

I Live Four Lives at a Time

BY ALICE THOMPSON

I LIVE a life of four dimensions—as a wife, a mother, a worker, an individual in society. Diversified roles, yes; but they are well knit by two major forces—an attempt to discover, understand and accept other human beings; and a belief in my responsibility toward others. The first began in my childhood when my father and I "acted out" Shakespeare. He refused to let me merely parrot Hamlet's brooding soliloquy, Lady Macbeth's sleepwalking scene or Cardinal Woolsey's self-analysis. He made a fascinating game of helping me understand the motivations behind the poetic words.

In college a professor further sparked this passionate curiosity about the essence of others and, by his example, transmuted it into a deep concern, a sense of responsibility that sprang not from stern Calvinistic principles but from awareness of all I received—and must repay with gladness.

I believe this acceptance, this tenderness one has for others, is impossible without an acceptance of self. Just when or where I learned that the full quota of human weakness and strength was the common property of each of us, I don't know. But somewhere in my late twenties I grew able to admit my own drives—and, rid of the anguished necessity of recostuming them, I was free to face them, and recognize that they were neither unique nor uncontrollable.

The rich and happy life I lead every day brings new witness to the validity of my own philosophy for me. Certainly it works in marriage. Any real marriage is a constant understanding and acceptance, coupled with mutual responsibility for one another's happiness. Each day I go out strengthened by the knowledge I am loved and love.

In the mother-child relationship, those same two forces apply. Words are useless to describe my efforts to know my own children. But my great debt to them for their understanding of me is one I have often failed to repay. How can I overvalue a youngster with the imagination and empathy and thoughtfulness to always phone when a late arrival might cause worry . . . to always know how to reassure? How can I repay the one who dashed into adulthood far too young but has carried all of its burden with a firm, joyous spirit?

My job itself is a reaffirmation of that by which I live. Very early in my working life, I was a small cog in a big firm. Emerging from a tiny job, I found a strange frightening world. Superficially everyone was friendly, but beneath the surface were raging suspicion, distrust, the hand ever ready to ward off—or deliver—the knife in the back. For years I thought I was in a world of monstrous people. Then I began to know the company's president. What he had been I have no way of knowing But at seventy he was suspicious, distrusting, sure that no one was telling him the truth; he had developed a technique of pitting all of us against each other. Able to see the distortion he caused, I youthfully declared if I ever ran a business, it would be on the reverse principle.

For the last two years I have had that opportunity, and had the job of watching people—widely different people, too—learn to understand each other, accept each other, feel mutually responsible.

My trials and errors have really synthesized into one great belief—which is that I am not alone in my desire to reach my fellow man. I believe the human race is inherently co-operative and concerned about its brother.

◄§ MRS. ALICE THOMPSON, publisher and editor-in-chief of the magazine *Seventeen*, is the first and only woman publisher of a national magazine in the United States. A graduate of Swarthmore College, she worked for Condé Nast Publications for eleven years, originating *Glamour* magazine and serving as its editor-in-chief for over two years.

All her many activities reflect her great interest in people, especially young people. Mrs. Thompson finds time apart from her publishing responsibilities to work in many organizations —the National Foundation for Infantile Paralysis, the National Conference of Christians and Jews, and the Save-the-Children Federation These activities stem from her belief in the obligation of the individual to society.

A Connecticut commuter, Mrs. Thompson runs her own home without help, cooks, cleans, and spends her few free minutes with music, and her two grandchildren.

My World Was Wrecked Once

BY ELIZABETH GRAY VINING

WHEN I WAS YOUNG I thought that beauty and courage and human love were the enduring values by which I could live. The beauty of nature, of an apple-green sky in a December twilight, of sunshafts through trees, of distant mountains, the beauty of words in poetry or fine prose, fed my spirit Courage—even a little of it—enabled me to face the disappointments that come to all young writers and to weather the disasters of the Great Depression. Human love meant for me a circle of friends and family and, above all, my brilliant and adored husband, Morgan Vining.

In 1933 he was killed in an automobile accident and I was seriously injured myself. I had nine weeks in bed to contemplate the wreckage of my world. I realized then that beauty and courage and human love, though indispensable, were not enough. During a long winter I sought desperately for the rock of truth on which to build my life anew and found it in the silent worship of the Quaker meeting. In discovering there the love of God, I found the love of neighbor infinitely widened and deepened. The realization that there is a spark of the divine in every human soul draws together people of all races, all creeds, all nations, all classes. This is why war is evil, and social injustice unendurable, why religion is incomplete without service.

I am a Christian, but I believe that all religions are pathways to God and become closer to one another as they mount nearer to Him. As William Penn said, "The humble, meek, merciful, just, pious, and devout souls are everywhere of one religion; and when death has taken off the mask, they will know one another, tho' the divers liveries they wear here make them strangers."

I have come to understand that we see only a small part of the whole pattern of existence. Sorrow and suffering give opportunities for growth. Disappointment often opens doors to wider fields. The tragedy of death, as someone wiser than I has said, is separation, but even separation may not be permanent. The sense of continuing companionship with those who have gone beyond the horizon which comes to me occasionally makes me confident that someday we shall see beyond the mystery which now we must accept. Often it seems that those who have most to give to the world are the very ones who are taken from it in the flower of their youth and vigor. It is hard to understand why this should be so, unless—and this I believe to be true—they have done whatever it was they had to do here, have fulfilled their secret contract with this world, and have been released for more important work elsewhere.

I believe in the power of prayer. I know something of this power through having been on the receiving end. After the war I was asked to be the tutor to the Crown Prince of Japan. In this fascinating but delicate and sometimes difficult work I was doing, situations arose in which I had no precedent to follow, no rules that I could consult. I had to depend more than I had ever done before on intuition. I used to hear again and again of people who were praying for me.

More than once I found myself lifted up and carried over the critical point, and it may well be that the prayers of unknown people in far places were helping me in ways I could not know. We understand very little about this power of prayer, and it is possible to misuse it even with the highest motives. I think that I can only ask that God's will be done in regard to any situation and that people whom I want to help may come to seek Him and know His love and truth directly. But by the very act of asking, if I do it sincerely and without reserve, I open myself as a channel for God's healing action.

᪥ ELIZABETH GRAY VINING, author of the best-selling *Windows for the Crown Prince*, has written a number of books for young people under the name of Elizabeth Janet Gray One of these, *Adam of the Road*, received the Newbery Medal for the most distinguished children's book of the year 1943. For adults she has written *Anthology with Comments and Contributions of the Quakers*

Windows for the Crown Prince is the account of her four years in Japan as private tutor to Crown Prince Akihito She was appointed Imperial tutor upon the recommendation of the American Friends Service Committee, with which she worked during World War II.

Elizabeth Vining is a member of the Society of Friends and has an immense respect for the worth and dignity of the individual. Tall and slender, she has dark hair and very blue eyes. She lives near Philadelphia in a quaint little house with an old garden.

What Would Christ Have Done?

BY CONSTANCE WARREN

I AM ONE of those very fortunate people who have loved my job, teaching, for I think it is one of the most important in this world. I believe that we must understand, in order to live richly within ourselves—and usefully to others. I am convinced that misunderstanding and suspicion come from ignorance, and I have faith that most young people are eager to learn and very discriminating as to the values for them of what one has to teach. I think we must all learn early to distinguish between pleasures and happiness and that happiness is the by-product of service. The key phrase in the Bible, to my mind, is "He that loseth his life shall find it." I have never been interested in theology, but the teachings of Christ seem to me basic to good living. I suppose I do just what most people do, clothe Him with all the finest traits which I have discovered in people I have known, and then, when I'm puzzled, I think, "What would Christ do under these circumstances?"

I believe strongly that we can never build happiness on the misery of other people, that the time is past when we can be content with relieving the misery in this world, that we must now focus our most constructive thinking and energy on eliminating its causes. The growth of this viewpoint seems to me the most encouraging development in a troubled world. Friendships are very important to me, for I believe strongly that human relations should be an inspiration to creative living. I am sure that, by and large, if I trust people, they will live up to my trust. I never look for trouble until it is thrust in my face. I also believe strongly that with deep capacity for affection should go equally deep objectivity, that it is absolutely essential to be fair with everyone. I never believe in competing with anyone but myself. I feel that that is the best way in the world to get the summation of my ambitions.

I think we are responsible for consciously training ourselves to so make comparison between our own situation and that of other people that we avoid self-pity. Suspicion and self-pity seem to me two of the most corroding characteristics which one can have, and I must be constantly on the alert to prevent them from getting a foothold in my thinking.

I believe that growing old should be a rich summation of experience, not a decay; that, generally speaking, we make of our old age a heaven or a hell and can look for no greater rewards or punishment in any future life than we can give ourselves in this one. Although a Protestant, I believe in the Catholic idea of a "treasury of good works," not laid up by saints alone but by anyone who has tried hard to live usefully and happily. I am not concerned that my name should be remembered, but I hope that I may have accumulated a little anonymous treasury which will filter down through succeeding generations and add to the sum total of right values by which men live.

◄§ CONSTANCE WARREN, a tall, active woman of seventy-one, is absorbed in education and world affairs She comes from a teaching family, and for years after graduating from Vassar and Columbia she taught history. For sixteen years she headed a new adventure in education, Sarah Lawrence College, where flexibility replaced the traditionally rigid curriculum.

Now president emeritus, she has five honorary degrees, and has written numerous articles and a book, *A New Design for Women's Education*. Her astonishing energy has also supported vigorous battles against racial prejudice She is chairman of the National Committee on Education of the American Association of University Women.

Miss Warren now spends nearly half the year in her ancestral home in Maine, reading, writing and working in crafts. As if in tribute to the durability of her convictions, her "This I Believe" credo was sealed in the cornerstone of the new Student Arts Center at Sarah Lawrence in the spring of 1952.

Goodness Doesn't Just Happen

BY REBECCA WEST

I BELIEVE in liberty I feel it is necessary for the health of the world that every man shall be able to say and do what he wishes and what is within his power. We must understand life if we are to master it; and each human being has a unique contribution to make towards our understanding of life, because every man is himself unique His physical and mental make-up is unique, his circumstances are unique. So he must know some things which are known to nobody else. He must be able to tell us something that could not be learned from any other source.

I wish I believed this only when I am writing about politics, but I believe it also in my capacity as a woman with a family and friends. I do not find it makes life easy. For if you let a man say and do what he likes, there comes a point when he wants to say or do something which interferes with the liberty of someone else to say or do what he likes.

Therefore it follows that I see the main problem of my life, and indeed anybody's life, as the balancing of competitive freedom. This involves a series of very delicate calculations, and you can never stop making them. This principle has to be applied in personal relations, and everybody knows that the Ready Reckoner to use there is love; but it takes a lot of real talent to use that effectively. The principle has to be applied in social relations also, and there the Ready Reckoner is the Rule of Law, as political scientists call it; a sense of mutual obligations that have to be honored, and a legal system which can be trusted to step in when that sense fails. When I was young I understood neither the difficulty of love nor the importance of law. I grew up in a world of rebellion and I was a rebel. I thought human beings were naturally good, and that their personal relations were bound to work out well, and that the law was a clumsy machine dealing harshly with people who would cease to offend as soon as we got rid of poverty. We were quite sure that human nature was good and would soon be perfect.

Yes, I remember that when I was something like eleven years old a visitor to my mother's home who had been in Russia described how she had one day been caught in the middle of a pogrom, and seen the Cossacks burning and looting and knouting the Jews in the street. I remember listening and thinking, "I mustn't forget this, people will be interested to hear of this when I'm old because of course all this sort of thing will have died out long before." You can imagine what a shock it was to me and my generation when that sort of thing became common form in many parts of the world, and such a pogrom, though horrible, seemed a small thing compared to the vast horrors committed on the millions of victims of totalitarianism.

Horrors which were committed by human beings like me I realize now that what is good on this earth does not happen as a matter of course, it has to be created, it has to be maintained, by the effort of love, by submission to the Rule of Law. But how are we to manage to love, being so given to cruelty, how do we preserve the law from being corrupted by our corruption, since it is a human institution? As I grow older I find more and more as a matter of experience that there is a God, and I know that religion offers a technique for getting in touch with Him, but I find that technique difficult. I hope I am working a way to the truth through my writing, but I also know that I must orientate my writing towards God for it to have any value It is not easy but I remind myself that if I wanted life to be easy I should have gotten born on a different universe.

Rebecca West was born on Christmas Day, 1892, in County Kerry, Ireland. Now one of the most noted women writers of our time, she began her career at nineteen as a reviewer for Freewomen. The next year she became the political writer for The Clarion. Since then she has steadily contributed to English and American publications.

Present at the Nuremberg trials as correspondent for London's Daily Telegraph, she was widely praised for her reporting. President Truman presented her with the Women's National Press Club's Award for Journalism for being "the world's best reporter." She also witnessed the Old Bailey treason trials which supplied material for her book The Meaning of Treason.

Miss West's other books include a novel, The Thinking Reed, and studies of Henry James, D H. Lawrence and St. Augustine. She lives with her husband, a retired banker, on their farm in Buckinghamshire, England.

Baseball Has a Religion Too

BY JOE WILLIAMS

THERE IS A SAYING at the race track that you can't "rule a man off for trying." I believe in this approach to life on this earth. I believe in God. I believe in my country. I believe in basic human decency I believe there is a right and a wrong way to do things. If I were asked to define Americanism—what made our country what it is to date— I would say it was the American's willingness and ambition to stand on his own two feet. I keep a box score on every baseball game I cover. There is a credit column in which hits are recorded and there is a debit column in which errors are listed. These are often deceptive. They will give hits to a batter who has been lucky and they will charge errors against a fielder who has been unlucky. This is a small mirror of life itself. These things over a long run even up just as they do in life.

I've seen shortstops make errors on plays another shortstop would not even try to make. He had his record in mind. The shortstop who made the errors had the team's success in mind. He was willing to sacrifice his personal record in the greater interest of the team's success. There is a kind of religion in that attitude.

I've often wondered how it would be, how it would affect the lives of our people if we all kept a daily box score on ourselves. As a matter of fact, I believe in sports as a way of life. It was Wellington who said battles are won on the playing fields of Eton. I believe it can be stated with equal truth that the principles of decent citizenship are born on the sand lots of Bass River, Massachusetts, Peoria, Illinois, and Southgate, California.

That's where our youngsters first see the religion of sports, if I may be permitted the term, in actual use. They learn about fair play, sportsmanship and working together in a common cause. And because they frequently learn by ugly contrast, their instincts and

189

the early teachings they got from their parents are sharpened against unfair practices, bullyragging and swell-headedness.

Not too long ago I had what was apparently a narrow escape from death. I was the last passenger out of a burning plane, the crash of which had instantly killed the pilot. I believe I am a physical coward, but singularly I felt no fear when I came to and began to seek a way to safety. Maybe I was still stunned, but I was completely composed. I did not pray, though I believe in prayer. I did not think of my family, though I am devoted to my family. I was neither sure I would escape nor that I would perish. I was, I suppose, completely resigned to whatever fate awaited me.

They have another saying around the race tracks—"The red board is up." This means the race is over, the result is final, and there's nothing anybody can do about it. It has gone into the records.

I believe that somehow much of the philosophy of the people I live with has rubbed off on me. I don't know whether this is good or bad. All I know is that is how it is with me and I've lived a happy life and I hope a reasonably decent one according to my lights.

JOE WILLIAMS, executive sports editor of the *New York World Telegram and Sun* and sports columnist for the Scripps-Howard newspapers, has spent his entire professional life writing about sports. This soft-spoken, peace-loving man somehow manages to be always in a fight, a fight against abuses and corruption in the sports world.

He feels deeply about the importance of sports as an influence on our way of life, but describes himself as "just a fan at heart." Mr. Williams put aside his great love of athletics long enough to head a committee for Finnish Relief under former President Herbert Hoover. His work was so successful that he was decorated by the President of the Finnish Republic.

A resident of Essex Fells, New Jersey, he commutes to his work in Manhattan. The sports story he likes best to tell is about the time he "scooped" the baseball world on Babe Ruth's resignation from the Yankees.

Maxie's Recipe for Happiness

BY MEREDITH WILLSON

I GUESS the creed of all human beings embraces the desire to leave their mark on the mortal world, when they pass to the immortal one. Maybe this is even the strongest of all urges of the human soul. Many men feel a fervent need to leave a son to carry on their name; noncreative people envy the Shakespeares and the Beethovens, as draftsmen envy the Frank Lloyd Wrights, and as the commercial artist envies the Rembrandts and the Raphaels. Maybe it's this kind of frustration that caused Henry Thoreau to remark, "the mass of men live lives of quiet desperation."

Well, I had a friend by the name of Max Terr. And Max taught me that genius is by no means an essential for escape from this "quiet desperation." Max had been associated with me as choral director for the past twenty years or so. Max was interested in almost everything; and considering that he was also a perfectionist, his interest was always a very intense one—even if it was only in a pencil.

Being a composer and orchestrator, he was constantly writing at the piano and he could see no reason to live with a clumsy pencil or a bad light, so he puttered and he searched until he found a graceful, dependable, thoroughly efficient pencil and a fine light for his work, completely comfortable and satisfactory in every respect. Now, Max very casually included his friends in this continuous research of his, and no one who knew Max ever took any of his suggestions lightly.

Since Max has gone, not a day passes that isn't a pleasanter day because of the things he left behind him. I have his particular kind of pencil in every pocket of every suit, on the desk, on the night table and on the piano. Couldn't live without 'em. I have the light with the flexible stand Maxie insisted I buy, so I no longer strain my eyes

We have the world's greatest cookies at our house which Max

sent one Christmas, after shopping all over town to find the best items to include in a basket for us. He found the cookies in a little shop as only he could patiently unearth such things. Now all our friends keep them around all the time. They call them "Maxie's cookies" without ever having met Max Terr.

"Tristram Shandy," Max told me one day, "is an old story with a tremendously inventive style. You like to write in the experimental forms. You have to read that book . . . it'll give you a lot of courage in doing things your own way"—and it sure did. Another day, he said, "The colors in your music room make it difficult to have just the right kind of a picture in there, but you know, Meredith, I picked up a print in a little art store that I think will just do the trick. Here it is. Take a look at it—didn't cost hardly anything either."

In every room of our apartment there are memories of Max Terr. And lots of our friends swear by his patiently discovered items, passing them along to their friends . . . praising "Maxie's cookies," "Maxie's music paper," "Maxie's pencils and piano light" without ever having known Max Terr. So I guess I believe pretty firmly that you don't have to be a Beethoven or a Rembrandt, or even a father, to leave a heritage to the mortal world. This is not a creed, exactly, nor is it a complete personal objective—or is it? Anyhow, I think if I leave behind me any part of the kind of things that keep Max Terr alive in the hearts of his fellows, I will have justified my brief hour of strutting and fretting upon the stage.

◄§ MEREDITH WILLSON, composer and musical director, began his career as a flute soloist with John Philip Sousa's band. Later he was a flutist with the New York Philharmonic Symphony under Arturo Toscanini.

Known to millions through his radio programs, this tall, black-haired native of Mason City, Iowa, has been with the National Broadcasting Company for twenty years. Some of the major radio programs with which he has been connected include the Ford Sunday Evening Hour, the Standard Symphony and, recently, the Big Show, and Meredith Willson's Music Room.

During the last war Mr. Willson contributed his experience to the Army as a Major in the Armed Forces Radio Service. His symphonic compositions include "Missions of California" and "Jervis Bay." Among his many popular hits are "You and I" and "May the Good Lord Bless and Keep You." On top of all this he is a successful author.

Two Commandments Are Enough

BY PEGGY WOOD

OCCASIONALLY my mother used to announce that she was going to take time out from the day's activities "to rest," she would say, "and to invite my soul." She always put the phrase in quotes, in order, I expect, to divert the facetious remarks which might arise from the worldly or practical-minded folk within earshot or to disarm those who might feel "soul" was a Sunday word not to be used in everyday conversation.

But she meant to do exactly what she said, "invite my soul."

The pressure of the modern world is so great upon us today that we find little time for rest, physical rest, let alone leisure for spiritual reception. Thus, when we take the word "soul" out of its Sunday clothes it is unfamiliar to us, we don't know it very well. We may have different interpretations of the meaning of the word; to some it may mean "conscience," to others that part of our being given us with life. I believe with Dr. Schweitzer in the sanctity of life, that the miracle called life, which cannot be manufactured by man, does come from a source which we call God, and that life and soul are the same. And yet when I am asked point-blank, "What do you believe?" I hedge and play for time in my confusion by saying, "Well, now, that's a pretty big question."

It is not altogether the pressure of the modern world which has clouded our comprehension; "the simple faith of our fathers" got a nasty jolt when Copernicus propounded his theory that the sun and stars did not revolve around the earth and that therefore man was not the sole object of celestial concern. Darwin dealt another blow and Freud's search into the operations of our hidden selves shook our conviction that man could be made in the image of God.

It might be said that such matters affect only dogma and not belief, and yet the mounting complexities of man's discoveries about himself and the world he lives in increase so with the years it is

193

little wonder man cries out for something simple and enduring in which to believe.

As in moments of great grief the reeling emotions steady themselves by concentrating upon small physical occupations—the careful tying of a shoelace, the straightening of a crooked picture on the wall, the tidy folding of a napkin—so I believe, in this heartbreaking world, in tending to the simple familiar chores which lie at hand. I believe I must keep my doorstep clean, I must tidy up my own backyard. I need keep only the two great commandments to live by: to respect the Giver of Life, and my duty towards my neighbor.

I believe that people deeply revere these two commandments (upon which hang all the laws and the prophets) and suffer personal distress when they are broken. When the property owners in South San Francisco refuse to let a Chinese family move into their district, when flaming crosses are burned and when the homes of decent people are bombed, we are all aware that our own doorsteps have been sullied and the human neighborhood besmirched.

If I am too puny to grasp the cosmic contours I believe I can at least live my faith within my own small orbit, gaining in strength from others until that time when all men can rest—and invite their souls.

*⋖§ Peggy Wood, actress and author, was born in Brooklyn. Often type-cast in mother roles, she was recently awarded the Royal St. Olav Medal of Norway, for bettering American-Norwegian cultural relations in her leading television role, "Mama."

Her father, a magazine writer who loved music, wanted his only child to be an opera singer. She started her career in the chorus of a Broadway musical. Six years later, she was a star, in Maytime. Between musical successes, she appeared in dramatic productions, including Candida, Blithe Spirit and Trelawney of the Wells. Her literary career started with a diary she kept while on tour with the late John Drew, which developed into a book entitled The Splendid Gypsy. She has published four other books.

Married to William Walling, printing firm executive, blonde, warmhearted and witty Peggy Wood commutes between their home in Connecticut and their New York apartment.

Philosophy from a Tugboat

BY GEORGE YOUNG

ONE NIGHT many years ago I was on the bridge of a ship that passed one of our large cities on a quiet night. I saw its lights reflected in the sky and heard the rumblings of the city's noises As I looked to my other side, I could see nothing but open space of darkness and endless water. I realized how small I was and that my own problems of life did not seem great.

I have spent twenty-five years on boats. Now I am a docking pilot. My job is to bring in the large luxury liners and stay with them until they are safely moored in their berths. Sometimes this requires two tugs, sometimes many more, depending on the tide, the weather, and the draft of the vessel.

Most of you no doubt have seen these tugs pushing and pulling at the big liners. What they are doing doesn't seem to make much sense, but presently the big boat is alongside her pier, her hawsers made fast, and the job is done.

These tugs, whether one or ten, move about in accord with whistle signals I send them from the bridge of the big liner. These signals make up a language that is just as dependable as the spoken word; or even more so, because our docking signals are rarely misunderstood. The captain of each tug does his work according to the signals he receives. He never asks questions. He takes everything on faith, and it always works out.

Working around tugboats, where so much depends on teamwork, has had its effect on what I believe. I believe that if I am to attain a successful place in the world I must have the help of my fellow man just as the great transatlantic liners depend on the help of the little tugs to bring them safely to port.

I felt very important the first time I ever docked a big liner. She came riding up the harbor on a flood tide and towered high over the stout little tug that carried me. As we drew alongside, a doorway

195

opened almost at water level and two smartly rigged sailors helped me aboard. I was escorted to the bridge where I took over from the captain. I realized I was in control of a great ship worth millions of dollars and the owners were depending on me to bring her safely to her berth. After I had docked several of the large liners, I realized I was not important, but simply the quarterback who called the signals.

In spite of what we read in the newspapers, I have a great faith in this country and I pray that a peaceful understanding will come to this unsettled world, so that my children can grow up in a world that will give them happiness instead of bloodshed. I believe this will come about. I remember the understanding and sympathy that took over this country, back in 1949, when a little girl named Kathy Fiskus fell into an abandoned well out in California. Engineers and sandhogs and people in all walks of life worked almost three days, and when they got her out she was dead. People sent in thousands of dollars in rescue funds, but those who did the work and furnished the equipment wouldn't take money. They worked for bigger stakes. I talked to captains of foreign ships that came into New York Harbor, and they were just as concerned as we Americans over the tragedy. I believe some way will be found to work together for world peace with the same sympathy and understanding that people worked to rescue little Kathy Fiskus. I believe God will someday bring this about.

◄§ CAPTAIN GEORGE B YOUNG holds the responsible job of Docking Pilot for the Moran Towing and Transportation Company of New York. Proud holder of a license issued by the United States Coast Guard certifying that he is a "Master and Pilot—unlimited tonnage," he received this distinction only after years of hard work and study. Every day he safely guides into their docks such ships as the Cunard Line's Queen Mary and Queen Elizabeth, the French Line's Ile de France and Liberté, and the vessels of the Holland-American Line

He lives a quiet life in Bergenfield, New Jersey, with his wife and four children and is a devout Catholic. Deeply interested in youth organizations, he shares the belief that the future of this country depends upon the youth of today. He keeps trim by working around his property and enjoys a game of golf—but says he hopes his ships never take the course his golf ball usually does

Walk Clean around the Hill

BY DARRYL F. ZANUCK

Now THAT I can look back across the years from the so-called vantage point of experience in two World Wars, travel throughout a large part of the world, and contact with many of the outstanding personalities of our time, it gives me a great deal of real reassurance each day to know that way down deep I learned some fundamental values when I was a boy in a small town in Nebraska.

I have found one thing to be so very true—the virtues I learned as a boy are still fundamental virtues. My point of view has changed, of course, over the years, and so has that of my friends, but so much of all this change of viewpoint is like a small boy gazing at a hill on the plains of Nebraska. The hill remains the same. The small boy only sees it from another angle as he grows up.

I have always tried to walk completely around every hill I have found in life since, so that I could get a view from every angle. This, I think, reveals the difference between honesty and cynicism. When you see the hill from every angle, you have a much better chance at keeping life in focus. When you only see it from one angle you run the very great danger of becoming cynical.

Two of the fundamental virtues that have been such a great comfort to me in my life, from the days of my boyhood in Wahoo, Nebraska, until now are loyalty and charity. There are other fundamentals I learned as a boy, but principally loyalty and charity.

Loyalty is not only just a term—it has been a way of life for me. I mean not only loyalty to my friends and family, but to the honest values on which our country was founded. And to me, this guidepost of loyalty of necessity means loyalty to one's own self.

When I was growing up, I rebelled against so many things, and fought against so many of the basic ideas of life—but I found after so much rebellion and walking completely around that hill on the

197

Nebraska plains, in my mind's eye, that these virtues had not been tested over the centuries in vain.

Charity is another rule that has been of great comfort to me in so many trying situations. Charity is something you must learn. I have have been very lucky in life because I have been in a position to give charity, and one should never expect any other reward from charity than the satisfaction it gives.

In taking part in any charity you must give from your heart. Any other type of giving is a terrible cheat on life itself.

Charity and loyalty are two things that have touched my life very deeply. They have been a source of tremendous satisfaction to me every day I have lived. This rule of loyalty has caused me to check back on the course of my activities at the close of each day, to be sure I haven't knowingly hurt anyone in my day's activities.

I have tried to repair any hurts I have caused before the day's end. This undoubtedly is very selfish of me because I have learned that this rechecking of each day gives me a good night's sleep.

In walking around the hill on the plain each day of my life, the virtues I see—whether I am in London, Paris, Rome, Cairo, New York, Hollywood or Wahoo, Nebraska—are always the same.

I am grateful for those old-fashioned virtues that I learned as a boy in Nebraska. And I hope I will have enough humility always to be thankful I was born in a country that gave me this chance at life.

◀§ DARRYL F. ZANUCK, a native of Wahoo, Nebraska, visited California when he was a young boy and immediately resolved to go into the motion picture business. His early movie experience included working for one of the studios for fifty cents a day.

He ran away from home to enlist in the First World War, even though he was under age. After the war, he sold a story to the old Fox Film Company for five hundred dollars. From then on nothing interfered with his movie work except the Second World War, when as a Colonel in the Signal Corps he produced, among others, the world-famous film on the North African campaign.

Now Vice-President in charge of production for 20th Century-Fox, he is the guiding genius behind all their pictures He is the only producer in Hollywood history to win the Irving Thalberg Award on three occasions. An equal achievement is his winning of three Motion Picture Academy Awards.

The Thread of Permanence

BY WILLIAM ZORACH

IT IS STRANGE how certain things make a great impression on us in childhood. I remember these verses by Longfellow.

> "Life is real! Life is earnest!
> And the grave is not its goal;
> Dust thou art, to dust returnest,
> Was not spoken of the soul."

And again:

> "Lives of great men all remind us
> We can make our lives sublime,
> And departing, leave behind us
> Footprints on the sands of time."

Of course, my generation was much more sentimental than today's youth but whether this was great poetry, it communicated in simple language a message, and made a lasting impression on a small boy.

When I was fifteen I had an imaginary guardian angel and when I went to the country to sketch on Sundays, I asked for guidance, praying that someday I would be a fine artist and paint nature as beautiful as she really is. What this little ceremony brought me was faith in the world and a belief in myself.

My faiths and beliefs have been badly strained. The Atomic Age has caught us in a web of fear. Our lives seem so impermanent and uncertain. There is such a waste of human potential, of things worth while in people which never find expression. I sometimes think it's a miracle that anything survives. Yet I believe that a thread of permanence runs through everything from the beginning of time, and the most valuable residue will survive.

I believe everybody has an urge to somehow spin his own life into a thread of permanence. It is the impulse of life. Some would call it the drive to immortality. Whatever it is, I think it is good because it gives purpose to existence. But purpose is not enough. Artists are supposed to be notoriously impractical, but for myself, I found I had to make decisions and plans if I were to try to create anything. I realized that I must approach life not only with a sensitivity, a perception of beauty, but with a feeling of humility and reverence.

My creed as an artist is to love life and liberty and the world of people. A man who works and loves his work is often a man dreaming, and the spirit of his dreams will find forms and symbols to express that dream. It is a wonderful feeling to create something. But today, I think there is a lack of power of communication. If people, not just artists, but all kinds of people, could only open their hearts and express their sorrow, their happiness, their fears and hopes, they would discover they had an identity with the main stream of life which they never saw before.

Sometimes fear and cynicism so grip our minds that we lose heart. Then I try to remember how the great artists of the ages had the power of expressiveness Theirs was the power to communicate, to exalt, to move the observer to joy or tears, to strike terror and awe in the hearts of men; not just to decorate or merely entertain.

If we can expand the boundaries of men's thoughts and beliefs, we will discover we all have creative possibilities—talents to make ourselves real identities as individuals, with a hold on the thread of immortality. If we can awaken ourselves to it, I am convinced we shall find that this is an alive and exciting age of adventure and experimentation from which a new beauty and a finer world will emerge.

WILLIAM ZORACH, born in Lithuania and raised in this country, is one of our foremost sculptors. Among his most noted works are his "Mother and Child" in the Metropolitan Museum and his figures of "Youth" in the Norton Museum at West Palm Beach.

He lives half the year in an old sea captain's house in Maine, and the other half in his Brooklyn studio, converted from a carriage house. A powerful man with shaggy hair and green eyes, Zorach usually works in overalls and lumberjack shirt, carving his strong figures directly in stone

Zorach has been an instructor for twenty years in the Art Students League of New York, and is the author of a book, Zorach Explains Sculpture Mrs. Zorach is a painter and their daughter, Dahlov Ipcar, is also a well-known artist.

THE Editorial Board, who run "This I Believe" in its entirety, have thanks to give to many for its development, dissemination, and usefulness

Our greatest thanks to the many hundreds who accepted our invitation to write the hardest thing in the world (600 words of one's beliefs)—with a special bow to the 100 co-authors of this book.

And then thanks ... to WCAU of Philadelphia for their pioneering in broadcasting TIB ... to the 196 radio station owners who later gave free time as a public service ... to the 85 newspapers which run TIB weekly, especially to Mrs. Helen Rogers Reid and George A. Cornish who published it first in the New York *Herald Tribune* ... to the Armed Forces Radio Service who broadcast TIB six times weekly on 140 overseas stations ... to Voice of America, especially Alfred Puhan, for translating and broadcasting TIB weekly in six languages . . to the State Department, especially Edward W. Barrett, Dr Wilson Compton, Charles P Arnot, and Thomas R. Nickels, for selecting TIB as a major State Department project, and for all the work they did in presenting it to the leading newspapers of the world in each of the 97 countries or principalities where the State Department has representation . . to BBC, especially Basil Thornton, for their interest and work in getting guests

from Great Britain, also for broadcasting TIB from England to Australia ... to the hundreds of educators who have worked on TIB for school use, especially the 100 who do use it regularly in class work ... to Help Inc., a charitable nonprofit corporation, who thought TIB worthy and supplied the money to make it possible ... to the hundreds who through encouragement, ideas, and work helped develop TIB, especially the early ones—Richard E Berlin, Dr Greville Haslam, Leslie R. Severinghaus, Erwin D. Canham, Carroll Binder, Dr. William G Carr, and many others ... to the many thousands who have written what TIB means to them ... to William S Paley and Donald W. Thornburgh who were at the birth of TIB and have been of inestimable help in its growth ... to the hard-working staff who have done a prodigious job, especially Ernest Chappell, Alice E. Colgan, Donald J. Merwin, Gladys Chang, Ralph Richmond, William L Thomas, Alice D Brown, Robert De Pue Brown, and Joseph W. Savage ... and last but not least, the TIB representatives in each of the 196 cities who have secured local guests and represented us in many ways.

Without this unselfish and hard work, "This I Believe" and this book would not be. This is very heartening to us—and greatly appreciated.

Milton Keynes UK
Ingram Content Group UK Ltd.
UKHW020718301023
431584UK00006B/438